DEATH
OR
CANADA

DEATH
OR
CANADA

The Irish Famine Migration
to Toronto, 1847

Mark G. McGowan

NOVALIS

A Manuscript Researched and Written in Conjunction with the Ireland Park
Foundation and the Ballinran-Tile Films Production, *Death or Canada*

© 2009 Novalis Publishing Inc.

Book Design: Blaine Herrmann

Cover images: Movie still from Ballinran Productions Limited (front cover, top); Entrance to Toronto, Library and Archives Canada (front cover, bottom); Ballinran Productions (front flap); Ballinran Productions (back flap, top); M. McGowan (back flap, middle); Caherciveen Famine Cemetery, Kerry, E.J.P. McGowan (back cover).

Business Offices:

Novalis Publishing Inc.
10 Lower Spadina Avenue, Suite 400
Toronto, Ontario
Canada M5V 2Z2

Novalis Publishing Inc.
4475 Frontenac Street
Montréal, Québec
Canada H2H 2S2

Phone: 1-800-387-7164
Fax: 1-800-204-4140
E-mail: books@novalis.ca

www.novalis.ca

Library and Archives Canada Cataloguing in Publication

McGowan, Mark, 1959
Death or Canada : the Irish migration to Toronto, 1847
Mark G. McGowan.

"A manuscript researched and written in conjunction with the Ireland Park – Foundation and the Ballinran-Title Films Production, Death or Canada." – Includes bibliographical references. – ISBN 978-2-89646-129-5

1. Irish–Ontario–Toronto–History--19th century. –2. Ireland–History–Famine, 1845-1852. 3. Canada–Emigration and _immigration--History–19th century. 4. Ireland–Emigration and _immigration–History–19th century. 5. Toronto (Ont.)–Social –conditions–19th century. 6. Toronto (Ont.)–History–19th century. –I. Title.
FC3097.9.I6 M32 2009   971.3'5410049162   C2009-900705-3

Printed in Canada.

We acknowledge the financial support of the Government of Canada through the Book Publishing Industry Development Program (BPIDP) for our publishing activities.

5 4 3 2 1   13 12 11 10 09

"Upon the whole I am obliged to consider the immigration of this year a calamity to the Province."

– Anthony B. Hawke
Chief Emigrant Agent, Canada West
16 October 1847

The Irish Labourers' *Pater Noster*

In Te Domine speravi
Give us this day our daily bread
Father in Mercy, hear our Prayer.
All hope in human aid has fled
We sink in deep despair

Our little ones scream out with pain
And clamour to be fed.
Father, they cry out to us in vain –
Give us our daily bread.

O'er the gaunt infant at the breast –
The mother bows her head.
The fount is dry, in vain t'is prest –
Give us our daily bread.

The eldest born, with hollow eye
And eager stealthy tread.
Would take the food we cannot buy –
Give us our daily bread.

We must not beg—he shall not steal
Though stores before us spread.
But we will work with earnest zeal
Give us our daily bread.

Famine hath laid her withering hand
Upon each little head.
Oh Christ! Is this a Christian land?
Give us our daily bread.

Thy will be done—Father receive
Our souls when we are dead.
In heaven we shall not pine and grieve
Or want our daily bread.

J.P.L. Walton, 29 December 1846
Limerick Reporter, 15 January 1847

Contents

Acknowledgements

This slender volume is not what I originally intended to write. When the idea was first conceived, I thought I would compile a day-to-day account of the Famine migration to Toronto so that visitors to the Ireland Park Memorial could put the tragic events of 1847 in a local historical context. After considerable deliberation, I decided that most Canadians, even those of Irish descent, had very little idea of what happened during the "potato famine" in Ireland during the 1840s, let alone the effects of the catastrophe on Canada. As I began to talk and lecture about these events, however, people revealed to me a collective popular memory of the causes of the blight, who was to blame for the Famine, and the commonly held belief of "that's where the Canadian Irish had their roots." Given the considerable historical research on the Irish in Canada, much of it sparked by Donald H. Akenson's controversial book *The Irish in Ontario*,[1] I chose to write an overview of the events with the intent of placing the Famine in its historical context, while offering a glimpse of Toronto history that is still relatively unknown to most of the city's citizens.

As I ploughed through newspapers and correspondence of the time, I became increasingly impressed by the stories of individual initiative and courage: Michael Power, Toronto's first Roman Catholic bishop, who died of typhus while serving the migrants; of George Grasett, MD, who lost his life as a result of daily contact with sick Irish migrants at the General Hospital; of Edward McElderry, the Emigration agent who met and dispersed the hordes landing at Rees's wharf—he eventually died of dysentery, leaving a widow and eight children. These stories needed to be told. As my research assistant, Michael Chard, and I dug deeper, new evidence of the human story of the migration came to light—lists of the sick and the dead, who had until now been forgotten by history. As a social historian I was compelled to bring their lives to the fore; their names are listed in Appendix C.

I would like to thank Robert Kearns and the Ireland Park Foundation board of directors for their suggestion that this project be undertaken and for their financial help for the employ of two research assistants. Michael Chard, the principal research assistant, pursued clues like an intrepid detective; he has all the instincts of Hercule Poirot, combined with the industriousness of a gifted historical researcher, and the offbeat, intelligent humour of Gary Larson. Without his assistance, this volume would not have been possible. Patrick McGowan provided needed computer expertise and transcribed the Convalescent Hospital Ledger into a machine-readable data sheet. When published, this ledger should prove invaluable to researchers. Pat also pieced together the list of the dead from the fragments that Michael and I were able to provide for him. We began with about three dozen names; our Appendix C now contains the names of over 660 persons.

Neil Sands completed some excellent work begun by Michael Chard in the records of St. James Cemetery, and assisted with compiling the new list of the Famine victims. Once again, my most trusted colleague in archives, Marc Lerman, allowed Michael and me to probe the riches of Archives of the Archdiocese of Toronto (see Appendix D); Nancy Mallet gave similar assistance in the archives of St. James Cathedral (Anglican). Seamus Beattie, my good friend, assisted me as I navigated through the records of Limerick City and through the vast historical papers of Theresa O'Neill, his late aunt, who was one of Ireland's most dedicated local historians. Our search for the Irish sailing ship the *Jeanie Johnston* has become legendary in Warrenpoint, County Down. I am also very grateful for the assistance I received from Dermot Foley, Tom Dwane, and Kevin Hannafin, who directed me to specific Famine sites in County Kerry. Dr. Victor Fennell of Camp, on the Dingle Peninsula, offered my wife and me invaluable assistance on one of Ireland's wettest days as we explored, logged and photographed Famine ruins at Killelton.

I would also like to thank Novalis Publishing, particularly Kevin Burns, former Editorial Director, English Books, who greatly encouraged this project at a time of my own despair. Since then, Michael O'Hearn and Ronald Albert have provided a steady hand in guiding the manuscript through various publishing hurdles. Most recently, Anne Louise Mahoney provided needed editorial expertise and has made this a much better book.

Finally, my heartfelt thanks to the Faculty of Arts and Science of the University of Toronto, particularly Deans Carl Amrhein, Pekka Sinervo, and Meric Gertler, who provided research assistance so that I could conduct on-site work in the libraries, archives, and back country of Ireland and in various Canadian archives.

My own family has always paid a price for the times when "Dad" was lost either in his head or in his books and papers. My thanks and love to my wife, Eileen, who worked with me to photograph and chart Famine ruins in Ireland, and to our children, Erin, Patrick, Brendan, Kathleen, and John-Francis, for their patience and forgiveness. In some ways, the work on this book recalled my own Irish ancestors, who set out from Cork and Kerry 20 years before the Famine and carved out a life for themselves in what was then the Queen's Bush of Canada West, now Huron and Bruce Counties, Ontario. Among these pioneers were four generations of Irish women, all but one of whom were widowed as young mothers, but who carried on, drawing deeply from their Catholic faith and providing the best for their families: Ann Crosby, Margaret Ellen McCarthy, Gertrude Anne O'Neill, and Elizabeth Anne Geisler (McGowan). Crosby and McCarthy intermarried with Famine migrants and the Famine Memory became part of their story, even though their own Canadian roots were in the pre-Famine period. Such individual cases provide a testament to the Famine event as being a touchstone for the collective memory of many Canadians of Irish descent.

The Ireland Park Memorial is a study in and of itself (See Appendix E). Conceived by Irish expatriates and supported by Irish descendants and members of many other ethnic communities in Toronto, the Park bears witness to both the immigrant experience and the way in which a host community rose to the enormous challenge it faced in the summer and autumn of 1847. The issue of "memory" has become a topic of great discussion among contemporary historians, in particular, the encounter between "collective historical memories" that are embedded in popular culture and the historical analysis provided by professional academics.[2]

The question of the Famine has been one in which historians, both traditional and revisionist, have faced the contradictory narratives that are loosely woven through the popular conceptions of the Irish experience in Canada and the sense of "Irishness" in general. Directors of the Ireland Memorial Park were careful in making certain that this Famine monument be situated within the broad context of the Irish migration to Canada, which began in strength in the eighteenth century, decades before the Famine. While this volume focuses on just one year, in one city, its intent is to encourage further social study of the Irish experience in Canada, while putting faces and voices to the bare statistics that have come to distinguish "Black '47" from the other phases of Irish migration. This volume is dedicated to the 1,124 victims of the Famine who immigrated to Toronto in 1847; in its own small way, this project has returned them to "memory."

Introduction
More Than a Moment in History

T he repeated failure of the potato crop in the late 1840s was the worst trauma to afflict Ireland in modern history. In the space of just little over a decade, over two million people simply disappeared from Ireland. In 1841, Ireland had a population of over eight million; by the time the next count was taken, close to one million people had died and over one million others had emigrated.

By 1861, the population of Ireland stood at 5.2 million, close to three million less than it had been 20 years earlier. Between 1845 and 1851 alone, it is estimated that 800,000 Irish people died and one million emigrated.[3] Whole villages were abandoned; others disappeared entirely, as did the surrounding farms, which were dismantled to provide pasture for herds of cattle and flocks of sheep. The Famine Period, 1845–1851, also witnessed an ill-fated rebellion, the dismantling of Britain's protective tariffs on the importation of foreign grains, the failure of the Poor Law to relieve the worst effects of the Famine on the starving masses, and an acceleration of the Irish people's resentment of rule directly from the Parliament at Westminster.

In recent years, the historiography of the Famine, as constructed by both Irish and non-Irish scholars, has spawned considerable debate about the nature of the Famine, the "nationalist" Irish interpretation of the tragedy, and the meting out of blame to those "responsible" for the huge loss of life and mass exodus from the island.

The Irish Famine is also a Canadian story. As many as 450,000 Irish migrants had already arrived in British North America (now Canada) before the first potato rotted in the soil of Ireland. Since the 1790s, Irish migrants had settled in Upper Canada's rich farmlands, built canals, established businesses in cities, and helped create the social and economic foundations of everyday life in this fledgling outpost of the British Empire.

Migrants from Ireland had been among the first European settlers of the colony of Newfoundland, the City of Halifax, Cape Breton Island, the Miramichi Valley, and Prince Edward Island. In the 1830s and 1840s, Irish Protestants and Catholics had hacked out sections of forest in the St. John River Valley, in New Brunswick, and had put their mark on such urban centres as Saint John, Quebec City, and Montréal. But the year 1847—known as Black '47—marked the high-water mark for Irish migration to British North America. Close to 110,000 people, most of whom were refugees from "the Great Hunger" (*Gorta Mor*, to the Irish) made their way to Britain's Colonies, and over 119,000 to the neighbouring United States of America.[4]

The Great Famine, from 1845 to 1851, however, was so dramatic in terms of the destruction of a way of life, that the memory of the Famine would become the principal touchstone of identity for Canada's Irish, whether they had crossed the Atlantic in 1847 or not. Since the 1980s, Canadian historians have spilled buckets of ink in efforts to account for the impact of the Famine on Canada and the resulting sweep of Irish migration to each region of the Dominion. The debate among historians has maintained a curious relationship with the "assumed collective memory" of the Famine experience to the Irish, their descendents, and others.

At times, revisionists have clashed and been rejected by holders of "the public memory," accused of belittling the suffering of the Irish or contributing to a professional cover-up of British misdeeds. At other times, historians and the public have been in agreement that the Famine must be properly commemorated and placed in the context of historic patterns of migration from Ireland. The study of the Famine migration, whether undertaken in Ireland or in the lands of the Irish diaspora, is not simple. From a Canadian perspective, studies and patterns will vary according to sources of migrants, shipping patterns, religious configurations of specific regions in Canada, numbers of Irish settlers, the relative wealth of the migrants, and the specific region of reception.

This book examines only one of the many regions of eastern and central British North America that experienced an influx of Irish migrants during what is acknowledged as the most significant year for Famine migration to Canada. Moreover, this book undertakes a detailed study of the Famine in Toronto, in full knowledge that the Famine migration had a significant impact on other parts of Upper Canada, Lower Canada, and the Atlantic colonies.

For Torontonians, in 1847, the influx of 38,560 refugees, most of whom were from Ireland, not only challenged public officials and strained local resources, but also the memory of "Black '47" would leave an indelible set of images on the minds of the local population regarding the nature and character of "the Irish." The city was not well prepared to meet the high proportion of sick and dying immigrants who would be forced to sojourn in this tiny burgh of under 20,000 people. Its location so far inland gave Toronto the advantage of being insulated from even higher numbers of those afflicted by "ship's fever" who would have to be cared for at the ports of entry or at Montréal, Kingston, and points in between.

Toronto's location also gave civic officials the advantage of having knowledge of what was happening in the eastern cities; this situation gave local officials the opportunity to avoid the mistakes made by well-intentioned but unprepared authorities to the east. While the Famine moment in Toronto brought out the best in many of its citizens and produced heroic acts from a few—including Dr. George Grasett, Bishop Michael Power, Nurse Susan Bailey, and Agent Edward McElderry, among others—the Famine also brought to the fore the underside of political infighting, small-minded patronage, fear-mongering, and bigotry, which can be so easily forgotten in the collective memory. Arguably, the Famine moment in Toronto marked the greatest challenge to face civic government in the city's young history; clearly, the government passed the test.

Second, the Famine moment shifted the city's demography to the extent that Roman Catholics of Irish origin and descent soon made up one quarter of Toronto's population. This fact would put severe strain on denominational relations in the city. In the case of those who remained impoverished, the new settlers placed equal strain on the city's charitable infrastructure.

Finally, the activities of "Black '47" placed an enormous burden on the local Catholic Church, which had lost its first bishop, leaving the Catholic community leaderless while facing staggering challenges to meet the spiritual, charitable, educational, and medical needs of its newest members. The Toronto story has many similarities with events as they unfolded elsewhere in the British North American Colonies in 1847, but it is not a microcosm of all that is significant about the history of the Famine migration in Canada. Toronto's experience is but one lens through which one region can be examined and assessed, with the hope of adding a few more pieces of the puzzle that comprise the Famine moment in Canada.

In many ways, this book is a response to the revisionists of the Famine. While they have been correct in stating that the Famine played a secondary role in the establishment of the Irish migratory and settlement grid in Canada, and correct that the Famine provided the high-water mark of Irish migration to British North America, those outside of the academy have read these conclusions differently. As would be revealed in the public hearings regarding the Department of Public Works and Heritage Canada's plans for Grosse Île, some Irish expatriates and descendents who spoke or offered briefs suspected that contemporary historiography was merely sweeping the Famine under the carpet. In so doing, the revisionists were playing into the hands of the "Imperial" conspiracy to absolve England of any blame.

This book is not interested in the question of blame. There was plenty of that to share: political ideologues blinded by laissez-faire capitalism at Westminster, detached and self-serving Anglo-Irish land-lords, self-interested farmers (Catholic and Protestant) with large diversified holdings, crooked ships' owners, parsimonious sea captains, ill-prepared colonial officials, civic corruption and patronage in Canada, and guilty bystanders who fled the scene when they could have assisted.

The incentive to blame could fill several volumes. Instead, this book endeavours to create an understanding of the Famine moment, its impact on the Upper Canadian culture of the time, and the assumed collective memory of the Irish and non-Irish thereafter. The revisionists may very well be correct in terms of historical geography, but where they sell the Famine moment short is in the psychological scarring it created and the images of the Irish that it engendered in the host community, the immigrants, and the descendents of both groups. These images could be resurrected for good, for ill, or for sport when the occasion demanded some explanation for Irish activity in Toronto or Canada. Numbers notwithstanding, the Famine memory, particularly that associated with "Black '47" became the defining moment of the Irish experience in Canada—by what was said and, perhaps, by what went unsaid.

CHAPTER ONE

Gorta Mor:
Roots of the Irish Famine

IN THE EARLY NINETEENTH CENTURY, the Irish landholding system, horticultural practices, and a population explosion provided the recipe for an agricultural crisis in Britain's oldest colony. Most of the rural landscape in Ireland had been carved up by Anglo-Irish landlords, at least one third of whom were absentee owners who left the care of their property to agents.[5] These estate lands were leased to Irish farmers, Catholic and Protestant, who often sublet their tenancies to small-scale farmers (cottiers) and agricultural labourers. Other farm workers (particularly in West Cork[6]) held parcels of land under one acre, or conacre, which entailed that they were compelled to negotiate annually with landlords and small farmers to lease these minuscule plots for their family's subsistence while they worked elsewhere. By the early nineteenth century, this landholding system was complicated by two factors: the rapid growth of the Irish population from around six million to eight million people,[7] and the interests of the landlords in maximizing their return from their estates by turning small farms into large pastures for the more lucrative livestock trade.[8] Terms of the leases, however, made the latter transformation very difficult, if not impossible on most estates.

Credit: E.J.P. McGowan

Annagh, Dingle, County Kerry

With this rapid rise in population a fact of life, Irish tenant farmers were compelled to subdivide their plots of land in order to ensure that their growing families, particularly sons, had a means of livelihood. As plots became smaller, Irish farmers became increasingly dependent on potatoes, which could be grown cheaply, provided high yields, and offered many of the essential nutrients required in the family diet. It was estimated that the average Irish farmer ate as much as fourteen pounds of potatoes each day.[9] It was clear to some farmers, particularly those with larger tenancies, that this landholding system and dependency on a single crop was not sustainable. The fragility of Irish agriculture and the precarious existence of its underclass of labourers and cottiers was reinforced by potato crop failures in both 1817 and 1821. It comes as no surprise, then, that the movement of people from Ireland to British North America began in earnest as early as the 1820s.

The first sign of disaster manifested itself in the autumn of 1845, when the fungus *phytophthora infestans* arrived in the rains from continental Europe and turned the potato crops in seventeen of 32 counties into a putrid mess. This blight had already hit parts of northeastern

North America, particularly New York, Pennsylvania, Nova Scotia, and the St. Lawrence Valley around Montréal, between 1842 and 1845.[10] On Cape Breton Island, for example, Scots and Irish migrant farmers, who depended heavily on the potato, endured a dramatic loss of their food supply in 1845, and many faced starvation.[11]

In Ireland, that same year, the fungus affected only the second harvest of potatoes. Many Irish likened this nasty turn of events to periodic crop failures experienced in the past, from which they had always recovered. Many counties remained unscathed and went about business as usual. The British government, under Prime Minister Sir Robert Peel, offered temporary stopgap measures, including food depots selling American maize in March 1846,[12] while local officials anticipated that the crops of the coming year would be sufficient to return the country to some degree of stability, as had been their experience in past crises. Maize, or dried corn, while an alternative food source to the potato, was unfamiliar to the diet of the Irish peasants. One of the broader economic effects of the failure of 1845, however, was Peel's repeal of the Corn Laws, the tariffs that had once protected British farmers from the import of cheap agricultural products from abroad. Support for Peel's actions regarding free trade were short lived. In June 1846, his successor, Lord John Russell, reduced large-scale relief, believing that the worst of the crisis was over.

Credit: M. McGowan

Ruins of Famine Village, Cil Reallig

Few could have predicted the events of the following two years.[13] By autumn 1846, the promising new crop of potatoes also failed. This time, the blight had struck nearly every county in the land. Irish farmers and the cottiers, to whom tenant farmers sublet land, were forced to eat their seed potatoes, leaving no hope for future planting. By early 1847,[14] starvation haunted much of Ireland, particularly in the western and southern counties, where the dysfunctional landlord-tenant system and subdivision of lands had been most palpable. With people having to spend more to purchase food, rent went unpaid. Some people left their farms willingly to seek out nourishment and work, while the agents of absentee landlords, with the help of the constabulary, evicted tenants who were in arrears when it came time to pay the rents that secured their tenancy.

The Irish problems were further exacerbated by the policies of Prime Minister Russell and the Whig cabinet and civil servants who answered to him. The Russell administration's eagerness to cut the outdoor relief efforts and distribution of imported food was motivated less by the promise that the crop of 1846 would be restored than by principles of laissez-faire capitalism. Charles Edward Trevelyan, the Secretary of the Treasury, was typical of the new breed of public official who had unwavering belief in the free market, which, when unfettered by artificial government controls, would right itself by means of natural market forces.[15] Ireland, Trevelyan thought, should neither be artificially propped up, lest the market be forever ruined, nor should regular shipments of other Irish grains and livestock be rerouted, lest the existing trade patterns be destroyed entirely. In addition, and perhaps on a moralistic side, Trevelyan and his like thought that extensive relief efforts would spoil the Irish people and make them forever dependent on government handouts. His public works programs would ensure, he believed, that the starving Irish would work for their daily bread.[16]

Some Irish landlords saw a silver lining in the crisis. Should the tenant farmers default on their rents and be forced from the land, landlords would now have the opportunity to turn the small landholdings into the much-desired pasture lands. Herds of cattle and sheep would soon replace that patchwork quilt of tenancies that had failed to be profitable to many who held title to the estates. On the Baltyboys estate in County Wicklow, for example, Elizabeth Smith, the wife of the local landlord, wrote eloquently about how her family aspired to such clearances:

> We determined to get rid of the little tenants and to increase the large farms—and we did it—but not at once—just watched for opportunities and managed this delicate business without annoying anyone—even causing a murmer [sic].[17]

Smith supported the government's shift in policy from public food relief to public works and the draconian clauses (Gregory Clause) of the Poor Law Amendment Act of 1847.[18] The Amendment effectively blocked public assistance to those tenants who held more than a "quarter-acre" of land; all relief would be distributed at the workhouses in the Poor Law Unions, and whole families would have to submit themselves to these institutions if they wished to eat courtesy of the public purse.[19] For Smith, this decision had positive implications for her estate: "The beggars are the small holders, entitled to no relief, and we shall gradually get rid of them; they must give up their patches and take to labour."[20] Smith's support of clearances appeared buttressed by her own loathing of the Irish tenants themselves, whom she described as being filled with "Envy, malice, evil speaking, hatred, lying, and all uncharitableness." In her diary she confessed, "How I do wish we had not one tenant in Baltiboys [sic]."[21]

Such ideas were not universally dismissed by a literate British public, who had already cultivated a rather negative image of the Irish, given the reports of indolence, poverty, and backwardness transmitted to them in travelogues and contemporary stories about Ireland. Several Protestant moralists had equally negative images of the majority Catholic Irish who appeared interminably wedded to the Papistical superstitions. Some had thought that the current food crisis had been a divine warning to the British government, which had just recently endowed a Catholic Seminary at Maynooth and in 1829 had effected the Emancipation of

Catholics by means of legislation that removed many of the political impediments placed upon Catholics by the old Penal Laws. God, in the minds of some government officials, had poured out His wrath for such developments and for the Catholic Irish's foolishness in wedding themselves to a single staple crop.[22]

Not all British observers of the crisis, however, shared this moralistic tone. The cheeky and unrestrained periodical *Punch* was assertive in its criticism of British policy in Ireland. Already having satirically lampooned Russell and his ministers since their assumption of power in 1846, *Punch* took dead aim at laissez-faire policies, finding them wanting in the light of Christian teaching:

> Lord Radnor is ready to die, at any moment, for St. Adam Smith and the blessed McCulloch. He wants the Irish peasantry to follow his example. His protest against the Destitute Relief Bill is a very powerful admonition to empty bellies not to grumble. Starvation is met by science, and death made demonstrably necessary. It must be a great comfort to Skibbereen to learn that nothing whatever can be done for hunger; that there are the most satisfactory reasons why Ireland should starve and England refuse to help her.

> We want a new Gospel of Political Economy for the use of nations in extremis. For "mercy," it should read "demand and supply;" and for "charity," "natural check." For "Do unto others as they should do unto you," the new Evangel must run, "Leave things to find their level." Where Christian law says "feed the hungry and clothe the naked," the Radnor dispensation substitutes, "Rely on your own exertions." For "Blessed are those that give," the new beatitude is, "Blessed are those who take care of themselves and leave others to do the same."[23]

Punch continued to support an expansion of relief efforts to Ireland, although it was highly critical of the persistence of the "Repeal" movement

Engraving from Illustrated London News

that urged dissolution of the Union between Britain and Ireland and the Young Irelanders who articulated it. Why, questioned the editor, are the Irish demanding Repeal, "yet they are rushing over to England in thousands every day[?]"[24] *Punch* was joined in its critique of the Irish landlords and government policies by *The Illustrated London News*, *The Times*, and some Radical members of Parliament.[25]

While the politicians and literati clashed, the situation in Ireland worsened. In the early winter of 1847, as food supplies dwindled for the common people, and as food prices remained high enough that even those persons of meagre means could not afford to purchase, the West of Ireland, already known for its recourse to violent protest during the crop failures,[26] simmered in anger and unrest. In January, in Adare, County Limerick, public works labourers, protested when the daily wage was reduced from ten pence to nine. The Viscount Adare called in troops who engaged in "striking and thrusting the people" with their bayonets. A serious riot was avoided when the local parish priest, Father Leahy, intervened and placed himself as a human shield between the soldiers and the mob.[27] Shortly thereafter, David Fitzgerald and his wife, an "an industrious and inoffensive" farming family living near Askeaton, in County Limerick, were brutally murdered with a hatchet, and their valuables taken.[28] In a similar act of desperation, seeking whatever money could come, a couple living near Youghal, County Cork, were arrested after they attempted to sell the corpse of their dead child.[29] In May, "drunken mobs" attacked food wagons on the turnpikes of Munster, and an unruly group of patrons smashed all the windows of St. John's Church Soup Kitchen in Limerick.[30]

As reports of violence in the countryside increased, so did the weekly lists of the dead and horrific stories of starvation that accompanied them. "Frightful destitution" was reported in County Clare, particularly parishes of Carrigaholt, Kilballyowen, Kilmacduagh, Kilmichael, and Cree.[31] At Skibbereen, in West Cork, shortly before Christmas, 1846, Cork magistrate Nicholas Cummins described the horrors that awaited him as he went door to door in the Parish of Myross to investigate the starvation first-hand and distribute food:

> I entered some of the hovels to ascertain the cause … and the
> scenes that presented themselves were such as no tongue or pen
> can convey the slightest idea of. In the first, six famished and
> ghastly skeletons, to all appearances dead, were huddled in
> the corner on some filthy straw, their sole covering seemed a
> ragged horse-cloth, and their wretched legs hanging about,
> naked above the knees. I approached in horror, and found by
> a low moaning they were alive, they were in fever—four children,
> a woman and what had once been a man.[32]

Between September 1846 and September 1847, as many as 7,314 people died in and around Skibbereen—just under 17 per cent of the population (Census of 1841), many of whom were buried in a mass grave at nearby Abbeystrowery.[33]

Similarly, reports from County Kerry indicated that there were so many dead per week that local gravediggers had exhausted the supply of coffins. As a result, the workers merely deposited bodies directly into graves without the dignity of a casket.[34] Three miles outside of Caherciveen, Kerry, on the Bothar Buí ("Paupers" or Yellow Road), just beyond the hulking ruin of the Bahaghs Workhouse,[35] lies a large walled field, tended to only by grazing sheep. This ruined cemetery is a lasting testament to hundreds of locals who died, their only marker being sharp flat fieldstones, stuck perpendicular to the earth, left without inscription by burial parties working in haste, without proper tools, and, perhaps, with minimal literacy skills.

The western counties of Ireland were not alone in their suffering. Crop failures in the Province of Leinster also spelled disaster for many tenant farmers and rural labourers. Writing to his son Patrick, who had immigrated to Nova Scotia, John Nowlan of Newtonbarry commented on the devastation evident in County Wexford:

> … your brothers are … all at present in good health thank god [sic] but knows not how for long for the people the young and the old are dying as fast as they can bury them the fever is raging here at such a rate that [they] are in health in the morning, knows not but in the evening may have taken the infection its like a plague the cause the doctors alledge [sic] is the kind of food being that yellow corn from America for the last year the potatoes were all blasted.

Credit: E.J.P. McGowan

Ruined Chapel in the Famine Cemetery, Caherciveen, Kerry

19

Nowlan added that he figured that not 20 barrels of potatoes had been harvested in all of County Wexford.[36] In his missive, Nowlan also confirmed the impression that the imported maize was an insufficient substitute for the potato, insofar as the Irish were inexperienced in how to prepare the dried kernels properly. If inadequately soaked or coarsely ground, the maize played havoc on the gastro-intestinal tract of those who consumed it. For many Irish, maize caused severe stomach pain and internal bleeding.[37]

Dissatisfaction spread to those men, women, and children who were engaged in the public works projects across Ireland. While poor wages and high food prices were at the heart of the disenchantment,[38] as was resentment towards the overseers and cheque clerks who managed the road works, the principal problem in Trevelyan's "work fare" solution was that those people already severely weakened by the Famine conditions were those least able to "earn their daily bread" by doing such heavy labour as smashing rocks and clearing thoroughfares. In February 1847, S.W. Roberts, reporting from the Barony of Farney, County Monaghan, vividly described the pathetic attempts of the poor to earn their food money in local public works:

> I cannot describe the poverty and destitution among the people of this barony; unfortunately the works in aid of relief were not commenced until the people were almost starving. Hundreds of them came to work without having tasted food for days before; the result was they were unable to earn wages capable of supporting themselves, and numbers of them left the employment in despair to go to the poor house.[39]

Roberts added that from December 5, 1846, to January 30, 1847, he had employed 9,608 men (at 10 3/4 pence per day), 7,042 women and girls (6 pence per day), and 3,606 boys (at 4 3/4 pence per day).[40]

Even if they were physically able to work, labourers found the wages too low to provide for their family. Many laid down their tools in protest or worse. As early as August 1846, 3,000 to 4,000 people gathered in Westport, County Mayo, to protest their wages; later, in October, on the

Knock Road, County Clare, a "check clerk" and an overseer were brutally assaulted by a gang. In December, on the Pullough Road, County Limerick, Private George Windsor of the Royal Sappers and Miners was attacked by "two armed men in women's clothes," in retaliation for fraud and corruption by officials on the road works.[41] In the fall and winter of 1846–47, disruptions in the public works were a daily occurrence across Ireland.

The result of the beatings, strikes, robberies, and vandalism by the "peasants" was always the same: the projects were temporarily "suspended." In January 1847, an inspecting officer in the North Riding of County Tipperary confessed that such suspensions would normally "remedy the evil" of idleness and protest, but "with the existing destitution, I conceive it to be a step which could not safely be adopted."[42] Modern economists, such as Amartya Sen, have argued persuasively that providing labour for people so that they may acquire money to buy food prevents both market collapse and dependence on government.[43] The problem in Ireland in 1846–47, however, was that such projects came far too late and people were unable to earn enough, because they were physically weak due to malnutrition.[44] In Killaloe, County Clare, however, the wages of poor labourers on the relief works simply could not sustain both their food purchases and rents.[45]

"… unfortunately the works in aid of relief were not commenced until the people were almost starving."

By early 1847, it was now clear to many observers, including some government officials, that the situation in Ireland was out of control. The Poor Law Unions and workhouses could not sustain the hundreds of paupers who clamoured for assistance. Charles Trevelyan's dictum of "Irish property paying for Irish poverty" was greeted with jeers from Irish landlords, some of whom found that one could not pay for social services if tenants were defaulting on rents and limiting the income of estates. The Poor Law Unions could not sustain the demand for shelter and sustenance.[46]

In February 1847, in Limerick, which housed Ireland's largest Poor Law Union, rate collectors were not able to meet their collections in full; several resigned. By March there were over 2,600 inmates in the Limerick workhouse.[47] By June 1847, with relief efforts strained to the maximum, the Russell Administration passed the Poor Law Extension

Act, which placed the burden of the Poor Law Rate on Irish landowners. With declining income, it was far easier to evict tenants who were in arrears than to underwrite the public relief.[48] In addition, the public works projects had failed miserably because most of the indigent workers were too weak to engage in manual labour, and the wages they received were insufficient to meet the cost of living and feed the destitute families.

Trevelyan ordered an end to the works projects, though the importation of maize continued,[49] but some observers continued to be baffled that the increasing imports of food did not translate into a lowering of food prices generally. According to the *Cork Examiner*,

> With this immense importation of food into the country, common reason tells us that there ought to be a proportionate fall in the market price of bread-stuff articles, or at least, if the prices continue high, the lives of people are not or should not be in the same perilous position from the ravages of the famine. Maize diet is yet high in the scale, and human life is lower than the usual average.[50]

Food, even maize, was still too expensive for the starving Irish, or was ineffectively distributed in the inland districts.[51] Desperate for food, people ate anything that appeared palatable. A story was told of a family at Ballina, Tipperary, who had to put down their donkey. Nothing, it was reported, was as miserable as seeing "a poor man salting down his ass for the consumption of his family."[52]

The soup kitchens, where hundreds could be fed daily, were increasingly used by churches and municipalities as a stopgap measure. In February 1847, the government provided support for these under the Temporary Relief Act.[53] Much has been written about "Irish souperism"; even more has been misunderstood. Quakers, the Church of Ireland, Presbyterians, and a variety of evangelical Protestant churches established relief kitchens as early as 1846. While Quaker establishments were usually beyond suspicion, rumours began to circulate that some Protestant-sponsored soup kitchens were using food relief as a tool for proselytizing the Catholic poor.

While this may have been the case in some relief establishments, it certainly was not the general rule. The Catholic Church itself supported and operated soup kitchens. In 1847, Archbishop John Ryan of Limerick not only donated to local relief kitchens in his diocese but, in January, established a "Soup Society" at St. Michael's Parish in the downtown "potato market" in Limerick City.[54] Similarly, the nationalist newspaper *The Limerick Reporter* endorsed these projects: "We heartily commend this important means of alleviating the sufferings of the poor to the charitable feelings and kindly sympathies of the affluent and middle classes … he who gives to the poor, lends to God."[55]

The fact remains that the bottom third of the Irish population, particularly those in the western counties in Connacht and Munster, starved.[56] In the Spring of 1847, parishes in the west began reporting their losses in the daily press. In May, Father J. Long, in the parish of Menheer, County Kerry, reported 160 deaths, of which he estimated that 106 came as a direct result of starvation.[57] Not far away, at Knockany Parish, County Limerick, Father John Ryan reported the deaths of 66 parishioners since October, most of which were caused by "diseases brought on from want of sufficient food."[58] Similarly, Father Andrew Quin, of Parish Kilfenora, County Clare, indicated that the 59 deaths that occurred in the same period among his people were approximately six times greater than that of the previous year. But of the living he reported worse: "Nine out of every ten living on insufficient food, a great majority of that number walking skeletons, barely existing, and falling victim to the slightest attacks of sickness."[59]

None of the aforementioned relief efforts succeeded in saving the population from destitution and starvation. Those with means made plans to leave their homeland in search of a better life. Those without such means, and they were legion, would have to take their chances at survival where they had farmed for generations. Father Quin's assessment of those who remained in his section of Clare was bleak: "Few have emigrated. There would not be 50 families in those two parishes in a month's time had they had the means to emigrate; our prospects for the coming year are gloomy … no potatoes sown here."[60]

CHAPTER TWO

Leaving Ireland:
A Summer of Sorrow

I N MAY 1847, *The Limerick Reporter* summed up the plight of its region's poor and starving: "In the present day there is a refinement on the edict of the Protector [Cromwell's famous ultimatum 'to hell or Connaught'], and the word is 'Death or Canada.'" The columnist went on to express grave misgivings about the mass migration of the Irish people:

> Nay, some very few honest men, but mistaken men, have espoused this wild and impracticable project. The grand inducement held out is, that death awaits the people in their own country, and they ought, therefore, to leave it as quickly as possible, without knowing whether as speedy as death does not await them in the wilds of Canada.

Canada, it was claimed, was a difficult country, both in terrain and in climate. The Irish in their "new Ireland" would "roam like a flock of sheep without a shepherd, indebted to a new landlord: the Land Company." The author then offered a better solution: exile the landlords to Canada and allow the Irish masses to remain, live, and develop their own country. As this item went to press, bread riots had erupted in Limerick when food carts were attacked by "starving victims of misrule" in the city's streets.[61]

Pundits and correspondents went back and forth on the pros and cons of emigration. Those wary of mass emigration may have had comments like those of Father Quin's in mind when they speculated that if only those who could afford to leave Ireland actually did leave, the country would be in a miserable state without those who "belong to the classes which continue to bear, not to increase, the burden of poor rates."[62] While the emigration of poor labourers would help to relieve the redundancy in the supply of labour, it was argued, the practice has been that emigration "tends to carry off a disproportionate number of those whom we can least spare."[63] Others, such as Arthur Neville Rolfe of Miltown, County Limerick, advocated shipping out the paupers, because "Ireland would be freed from a vast surplus population, which she cannot support; and those now in a state of dependence would soon … be able to send back their abundance to their own country." [64]

The case for emigration was supported by letter writers from Canada who urged their countrymen to join them. In one case, "T.E.," formerly of Limerick and now residing in Oakville, Canada West, indicated that Canada had large, unused tracts of cheap fertile land, excellent wages for labourers, "freedom from taxation, the use of the English language, and laws and institutions akin to those in Great Britain and Ireland."[65] Other reports made helpful suggestions about what to pack when preparing for the voyage, how to convert one's currency, the higher land rents, or what to expect regarding local foodstuffs in Canada, including encouraging reviews of the "Plums, apples, and pears in endless variety, and almost unlimited quantity," that grow in Upper Canada.[66] Those who could read the local papers, or were told stories of the promise of the colonies, were ensnared in a push-pull movement to leave: pushed by conditions in Ireland and the negative disposition demonstrated towards them by the elite, and pulled by the alleged successes of their countrymen in Canada.

The vast majority of the displaced cotters and labourers, however, had little choice about how to survive. The poorest died where they had lived; those with some means, or the assistance of their landlords, eventually flooded into England and Scotland; and others, with greater means, made the more expensive and more dangerous journey to the United States, Australia or Canada. In 1847, the worst year of the Famine to that point, 441 ships landed in Québec carrying as many as 80,000 of the nearly 100,000 emigrants, mostly Irish, who would venture to British North America in search of refuge.[67]

Despite popular myths to the contrary, only 6,000 of the migrants who set out for the Port of Québec were subsidized by their landlords.[68] Somehow, the vast majority of the Irish destined for Canadian shores had scraped up enough money themselves, or had received remittances from friends and family in "America,"[69] to pay for their passage and provisions while on board ship. Fares for the journey varied from port to port and also depended on the quality of travel. A person departing Liverpool for Québec would spend £5 10 shillings for passage "with full allowance of provisions," or £3 if he was willing to carry his own provisions beyond the legal allowance of water and meat to be provided from the ship's stores. The fares from Ireland to Québec were cheaper; the scale in Cork ranged from £5 for full allowance to £3 5 shillings for legal allowance, and in Dublin from £4 10 shillings for full allowance to a mere £3 for legal allowance. Children between the ages of one and fourteen travelled at half price, while infants were given passage for free.[70]

In the Spring of 1847, those Irish of even the smallest means flocked to Ireland's ports in anticipation of catching a boat out of starvation. The port of Dublin became the most popular point of departure for those taking advantage of the few shillings' fare to Liverpool, England. Once in England, migrants could sojourn with friends and family in the cities, either seeking work in local industry or on railway construction and other public works. Thousands of those who arrived in Liverpool took the opportunity to board one of the 72 ships bound for Québec that season. Similar stories unfolded in Glasgow, Scotland, where Irish migrants bought passage on 30 ships sailing to Québec, and in London, where Irish migrants were prominent among passengers on the nineteen ships sailing to Québec.

In Ireland, Limerick, Cork, Dublin, and Sligo were the most popular

The case for emigration was supported by letter writers from Canada who urged their countrymen to join them.

points of departure for Canada, collectively providing 157 ships bound for Québec that season. Other Irish ports witnessed a dozen or more sailings that season. In fact, of the 441 aforementioned ships landing in Québec in 1847, all but 36 came from ports in the United Kingdom.[71]

Table 1: Major Irish Ports and Migration, 1847[72]

Port	Ships	Total Cabin Steerage	Average Per Ship	Assisted	Percentage Assisted	Ratio X:1	Sick Average	Dead at Sea
Limerick	50	9,174	183.5	1,287	21.06	7.1	4.0	4.2
Cork	33	10,322	312.8	680	11.13	15.2	50.3	26.9
Dublin	27	6,568	243.3	2,079	34.03	3.2	18.8	8.9
Sligo	26	5,732	220.5	802	13.12	7.2	14.9	14.2
Belfast	21	6,913	329.2	5	0.07	1382	10.1	6.7
New Ross	15	4,395	293	251	5.71	17.5	16.1	7.8
Waterford	14	3,050	217.9	64	2.10	47.7	4.6	2.6
Derry	11	3,526	320.6	156	4.41	22.6	18.4	5.6

Table 2: Major British Ports and Irish Migration, 1847

Port	Ships	Total Cabin Steerage	Average Per Ship	Assisted	Percentage Assisted	Ratio X:1	Sick Average	Dead at Sea
Liverpool	72	27,039	375.5	512	1.9	528	43.4	25.8
Glasgow	30	2,019	67.3	0	0.0	0	2.7	2.0
London	19	1,985	104.5	0	0.0	0	0.3	3.3

The city of Limerick, for example, witnessed the departure of 50 ships, the largest number of ships destined for Québec from any Irish port that year. This region of southwest Ireland was in dire straits by 1847. As indicated earlier, violence was rampant in the countryside as dispossessed farmers and labourers battled local authorities for food. The homes of more affluent farmers were attacked, sacked, and, in some cases, the homeowners were murdered. Conveniently located where the River Shannon widens, Limerick City proved to be a magnet for would-be migrants: Catholic and Protestant Irish travelled by foot or cart from the depressed parishes of Limerick County, Clare, northern Cork, Kerry, or northern Tipperary en route to the region's chief port.[73] Others boarded boats, steamers, and ferries along the Shannon at Scariff, Ballina, Killaloe, or villages along Lough Derg, all of which offered quick and safe passage down the river to Limerick, where refugees hoped to find space on a boat to "America." In the Parish of Killaloe, County Clare, for example, the population dropped from 8,500 persons in 1845 to 5,606 persons in 1851. The tiny townland of Carrowna-gowan, within the parish, lost 87 of its 93 occupants.[74]

Advertisement of Sailing Vessels, Limerick to Québec, 1847

Limerick, much like other Irish port cities, tended to attract potential migrants from a huge local catch basin, making the demography of the Famine migration to Canada much more diverse, in terms of counties of origin, than previous waves of Irish migration. In the early nineteenth century, emigrants from the counties of Waterford, Wexford, south Tipperary, and east Cork had dominated the settlement of Nova Scotia and Newfoundland. Similarly, due to the connectedness of the ports on either side of the Atlantic, migrants from Ulster and Cork arrived by the thousands at Québec and Saint John, New Brunswick. The majority of these migrants were Protestant.

In "Black '47," the variety of the ports of departure from Ireland and the already diverse nature of the Irish population of Liverpool made for a rich mosaic of Irish newcomers, particularly from the western counties, where the Famine was most pronounced. In the absence of passenger lists, the actual breakdown of counties-by-origin is rather difficult to ascertain.

Nevertheless, the records of 1847 of the Grosse Île Orphans and those of Orphans in Montréal, when combined with the burial and the marriage registers from Toronto's Catholic parishes, offer a glimpse of the diversity of origins of Famine migrants who arrived in the interior colonies.

These routinely generated sources demonstrate a prominence of migration from counties in the provinces of Munster and Connaught. In the orphans records from Grosse Île, 23 per cent of children claimed origins in County Roscommon, which had suffered 40,000 to 50,000 deaths per annum during the Famine.[75] Most of these orphans were likely from the Estates of Major Denis Mahon of Strokestown, who subsidized the passage of 982 tenants on four vessels departing from Liverpool: the *Virginius, Erin's Queen, Naomi,* and *John Munn.* On the *Virginius* alone, 267 of 476 passengers (56 per cent) died at sea or in quarantine, after a journey that lasted 63 days at sea and 13 in quarantine.[76] With a legacy of evictions and misery on his properties, it is perhaps not surprising that, on November 2, 1847, Denis Mahon was felled by an assassin's bullet near Four Mile House, Doorty, close to his estates.[77]

In addition to Roscommon, other heavily represented counties included Tipperary, Loais, and Fermanagh, each of which experienced 20,000 to 30,000 deaths per year.[78] Similarly, the marriage registers of the Catholic Diocese of Toronto recorded both the birth counties of the betrothed and, often, the birthplaces of the parents of the bride and groom. Assuming that between 1847 and 1852 many of these couples were migrants during the Famine period, once again the western and southern counties appear very well represented.

Table 3: Orphans of Grosse Île and Montréal, 1847[79]

County	Province %	Orphans Grosse Île	Percentage	Orphans Montréal	Percentage
Armagh	Ulster	10	4.0	–	
Derry	Ulster	3	1.2	–	
Down	Ulster	–	–	3	3.5
Fermanagh	Ulster	19	7.7	5	5.9
Tyrone	Ulster	15	6.1	–	
Antrim	Ulster	–	–	2	2.4
Cavan	**Ulster 19**	–	–	2	2.4 (14.2)
Galway	Connacht	6	2.4	4	4.7
Leitrim	Connacht	–	–	4	4.7
Mayo	Connacht	15	6.1	3	3.5
Roscommon	Connacht	55	22.2	2	2.4
Sligo	**Connacht 34.7**	10	4.0	3	3.5 (18.8)
Clare	Munster	6	2.4	3	3.5
Cork	Munster	11	4.5	6	7.1
Kerry	Munster	–	–	2	2.4
Limerick	Munster	6	2.4	1	1.2
Tipperary	Munster	33	13.3	16	18.8
Waterford	**Munster 23.4**	2	.8	–	(33.0)
Carlow	Leinster	–	–	4	4.7
Kildare	Leinster	17	6.9	1	1.2
Kilkenny	Leinster	9	3.6	6	7.1
Loais	Leinster	20	8.1	6	7.1
Longford	Leinster	–	–	6	7.1
Meath	Leinster	7	2.8	–	–
Offaly	Leinster	4	1.6		
Westmeath	Leinster	–	–	2	2.4
Wexford	Leinster	–	–	3	3.5
Wicklow	**Leinster 23**	–	–	1	1.2 (34.3)
Total		248	100.00	85	100.00

Table 4: Marriages and Deaths, Toronto's Catholic Irish, 1847-52[80]

County	Province	Deaths	Percentage	Marriage[81]	Percentage
Antrim	Ulster	1	1.1	8	6.5
Armagh		3	3.3	13	10.5
Cavan		–	–	7	5.5
Derry		1	1.1	8	6.5
Donegal		1	1.1	19	15.3
Down		2	2.2	4	3.2
Fermanagh		5	5.5	26	21.0
Monaghan		8	8.8	23	18.6
Tyrone		2 (23)	2.2 (25.3)	16 (124)	12.9
Galway	Connacht	3	3.3	35	28.9
Leitrim		2	2.2	15	12.4
Mayo		5	5.5	33	27.3
Roscommon		3	3.3	8	6.6
Sligo		5 (18)	5.5 (19.8)	30 (121)	24.8
Clare	Munster	4	4.4	106	24.2
Cork		10	11.0	81	18.5
Kerry		6	6.6	49	11.2
Limerick		8	8.8	99	22.6
Tipperary		5 (33)	5.5 (36.3)	83	18.9
Waterford		0	–	21 (439)	4.8
Carlow	**Leinster**	–	–	7	2.8
Dublin		–	–	16	6.4
Kildare		2	2.2	16	6.4
Kilkenny		1	1.1	33	13.2
Laois		4	4.4	14	5.6
Longford		1	1.1	3	1.2
Louth		1	1.1	0	0.0
Meath		2	2.2	9	3.6

County	Province	Deaths	Percentage	Marriage[81]	Percentage
Offaly		–	–	26	10.4
Westmeath		–	–	10	4.0
Wexford		3	3.3	73	29.2
Wicklow		3 (17)	3.3 (18.8)	43 (250)	17.2
Total		91	100.0	934	
No County		55			

The ships that carried migrants had not been designed for passenger travel. Prior to their arrival in port in 1847, these three-masted sailing vessels had hauled cargo: grain from Italy, corn from New York, and timber from Québec.[82] Upon arrival in the Irish and British ports, these cargo ships were quickly refitted to carry hundreds of passengers as "human ballast" across the Atlantic. After the purchase of passage, migrants were given a cursory inspection by an attending physician. If their gums and tongues proved not to show signs of infection, they were herded into the awaiting vessels. Despite the advertisements claiming such things as "fine height between the decks and affords good ventilation," as the *Horatio* did prior to sailing from Limerick in July 1847, most passengers were crowded into the ship's steerage, where whole families shared single wide berths that were stacked three high. The *Guide to Emigrants*, published by the Board of Colonial Land and Emigration Commissioners, recommended that although the voyage to Québec was approximately 46 days, ships were required to provision water and meat for 70 days, in the event of an extended passage due to weather and currents. Irish and Scots passengers were advised to bring adequate supplies of bacon, red herring, oatmeal, sugar, tea, and butter, in addition to two pounds of soap. Passengers were also warned that they were responsible for cleaning between the decks, cooking in an orderly fashion, and obeying the Captain's prescribed times for bed and rising.[83]

The references made to such voyages in the *Guide to Emigrants* did not reflect the realities of the journey. The six- to eight-week voyage across the Atlantic often meant great discomfort; rough seas would ensure passengers remained cramped below decks, trapped amid the stench of food odours (cooking was allowed on deck only when weather permitted), stale air, and human effluent. James Attridge, master of the Québec-built *Jeanie Johnston*, warned passengers that no fighting, drinking, open flame, swearing, gambling, or spitting would be permitted below decks.[84]

Under these cramped and unhealthy conditions, death stalked these ships. On average, ships from Liverpool lost 26 passengers en route (the aforementioned *Virginius* was among the worst); from Cork, 27; but from Limerick, where local port officials were accredited with high standards of health and safety before sailing, only four per ship on average died during the voyage. The *Horatio*, for example, spent 45 days at sea, with 277 passengers, with a loss of eleven persons—nearly twice the average number of deaths on ships hailing from Limerick. Two weeks later, the *Superior* arrived at Québec from Derry, betraying its name in most categories: it had taken 51 days to make the passage, witnessed the death at sea of eighteen of its 377 passengers, and 21 additional deaths at the quarantine, in both cases far exceeding the averages for the Port of Derry.[85]

Several passengers and observers recorded their thoughts and experiences for public consumption, to improve the wretched conditions faced by Irish emigrants bound for "America." Stephen De Vere, an Irish landowner in County Limerick, convert to Catholicism, and nephew to Lord Mounteagle, made the startling passage to judge for himself the conditions on board the "fever ships." In a Letter to Lord Grey and later to a Select Committee of the British Parliament, De Vere would report:

> Before the emigrant has been a week at sea he is an altered man. How can it be otherwise? Hundreds of poor people. Men, women and children of all ages, from the driveling idiot to the babe just born, huddled together without light, without air, wallowing in filth and breathing a fetid atmosphere, sick in body, dispirited in heart, the fevered patients lying between the sound, in sleeping places so narrow as almost to deny them the power of indulging, by a change of position, the natural restlessness of the disease.[86]

Another account of a similar voyage was published by an elusive figure, Robert Whyte, who was allegedly the only cabin passenger on an unnamed vessel that arrived at Grosse Île. While Whyte remains a man of mystery, as does much about the identity of his ship, there is sufficient evidence to conclude that the vessel may have been the *George*, which arrived at Quebec on August 3, after a 64-day journey from Dublin that cost the lives of eleven of its 104 passengers. Should Whyte's comments be authentic, they offer a macabre tale of the effect of disease on board ship. Describing the deterioration of a female passenger, he writes,

> Her head and face were swollen to a most unnatural size; the latter being hideously deformed. I recollected remarking the clearness of her complexion when I saw her in health … now how sadly altered! Her cheeks retained their ruddy hue, but the rest of her distorted countenance was of a leprous whiteness."[87]

Based on such testimony, at the end of the shipping season, Canadians demanded improvements in the Imperial regulations for passenger travel.[88]

Typhus, or "ship's fever," had become the most common disease contracted on the journey, particularly on board filthy vessels, where nutrition, health care, and sanitation were substandard. This bacterial infection (*rickettsia prowazecki*) was transmitted by body lice, which, after having bitten the victim would defecate in the wound, passing the microbe and its toxins into the bloodstream. After an incubation period of a week to ten days, victims would suffer all order of headaches, rashes, intense thirst, enlarged liver and spleen, and skin eruptions. The infection ran its course within two weeks of appearance; the result was often tragic. In these times before the advent of antibiotics, which are now used to treat the condition, half to three quarters of those afflicted by typhus in 1847 died.

Canadian authorities, urgently trying to shield citizens from the contagion, demanded that all ships stop at Grosse Île, a quarantine station in the St. Lawrence River, 40 kilometers northeast of Quebec City; on the island, the healthy would be inspected and moved on.

Credit: M. McGowan

Interior of Lazaretto at Grosse Île

Incoming vessels were refused the right of passage to Québec until medical inspectors boarded the ships and examined the passengers. Those showing signs of the infection or advanced cases of "ship's fever" were removed to the island. The sick would be landed for treatment and convalescence and the dying for tending and, eventually, burial.

Grosse Île had not been prepared for what it would witness in the months of navigation in 1847. Dr. George Mellis Douglas, the physician in charge of the station, had been informed that he could expect 34 vessels in the early spring carrying 10,636 passengers.[89] At the time, both Douglas and the Canadian government were confident that the improvements to the station, suggested by Douglas at the end of the 1846 season, would be sufficient to meet elevated immigration levels. Douglas had expanded the facility from 150 beds to 200 and had recruited a staff of nurses, orderlies, and police;[90] he felt that with the regular hospital staff, in addition to the new sheds or lazarettos on the island, they could handle the situation.

The first ship of the season, *Cambria*, which sailed out of Glasgow, arrived at Québec without needing to stop at the quarantine. Neither did the next five arrivals; Douglas and the civic authorities were proved right.

The arrival of the *Syria* from Liverpool on May 20, however, blasted them from their complacency and proved to be a harbinger of darker things to come. After a passage of 46 days, which was marked by the death of nine passengers, the remaining 233 migrants aboard the ship were in horrendous condition. The sick were unloaded from the boats and placed in the sheds. Forty more passengers died. The *Syria* proved to be the thin edge of the wedge. Hundreds more ships arrived in the spring and summer, sometimes stacked up in long columns in the St. Lawrence waiting for inspection and clearance. New sheds for the hundreds of sick had to be constructed. Inmates died by the score, often having expired while sharing bunks with those still suffering or convalescing. By the end of the sailing season, over 5,424 migrants died at Grosse Île and were buried in its two cemeteries.[91]

Credit: M. McGowan

Celtic Cross Commemorating Famine Dead at Grosse Île, erected in 1909

Equally tragic was the fact that many persons who carried the infection in its incubation stages were cleared from the quarantine station because they had demonstrated all the outward appearance of health; by the time these migrants reached Quebec City, Montréal, Bytown (now Ottawa), Kingston, and Toronto, their symptoms began to show. In this way, the epidemic spread throughout Canada.

The cases of typhus were particularly severe in Montréal. Local authorities built "fever sheds" by the St. Lawrence River at Point St. Charles to house the sick. In a joint effort, the City of Montréal, the Canadian government, the Catholic Church, and such religious orders as the Sœurs de la Charité (Grey Sisters) tended to the migrants and suffered with them. Several priests, including Vicar General Hyacinthe Hudon, and nursing sisters contracted typhus themselves and died as a result.[92] On August 7, Sister McMullen informed Montréal's Catholic bishop, Ignace Bourget (who had also contracted the disease, but lived to tell the tale),[93] that of the 36 Grey Sisters attending to the Irish in the fever sheds, 28 had contracted typhus, of whom seven had died.[94]

Black Rock, Point St. Charles, Montréal

Credit: E.E. McGowan

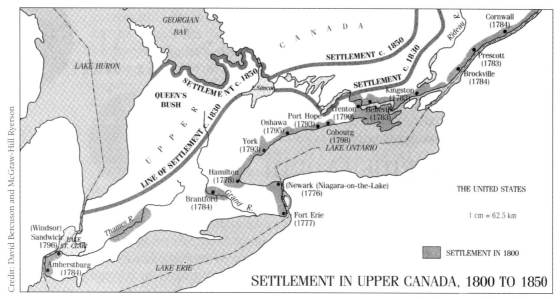

Credit: David Bercuson and McGraw-Hill Ryerson

SETTLEMENT IN UPPER CANADA, 1800 TO 1850

Settlement in Upper Canada

In 1859, local construction workers who were laying the foundations of the Victoria Bridge at Point St. Charles discovered the human remains of hundreds of the 3,300 Irish[95] who had perished in Montréal in the summer of 1847. In memory of these victims, the workers, in conjunction with the local Irish community, erected "the Black Rock" memorial as a testimony to those who had suffered so long in Ireland only to end their days abruptly upon arrival in Canada.[96]

The port of Montréal became the principal dispersion point for the Irish migrants, many of whom had never intended to remain in Canada. Since fares to British North American ports were cheaper than fares to the United States, and since many of the American tidewater ports levied high per capita taxes on ships' captains who landed anyone entering showing signs of illness, Canada became the first stop for the Irish diaspora. From Montréal, some migrants headed south to the United States to elude the border restrictions,[97] while others moved on to Upper Canada to search for relatives and friends, to stake out a new home in an unknown wilderness, or with the intention of moving to American vistas farther west: Buffalo, Ohio, Michigan, and the territories of the American midwest.

In March 1847, for example, Daniel McNamara, a native of Limerick who had recently immigrated to Upper Canada, wrote to Bishop Ryan indicating that he had spent two months in Ohio in 1846 engaged in a futile search for his brother. Despite his suspicion that Ohio held out better opportunities than the northern colonies did, he returned to his family in Richmond Hill.[98]

As had been the case in Montréal, however, other Canadian towns farther inland experienced the signs and relapses of typhus as Irish migrants poured inland. Transportation by steamer was only 30 hours from Lachine to Kingston, if one had the means. For many Irish migrants, the landing in the former Canadian capital of Kingston would be their last. By season's end, the citizens of Kingston witnessed at least 700 deaths in the hastily erected sheds at King and Emily Streets in the downtown core of the city.[99] For those healthy migrants, or those in whom the disease had been undetected, the journey continued up the St. Lawrence and into Lake Ontario, with the anticipated destination being Cobourg, Port Hope, Port Windsor (Whitby), Toronto, or Hamilton. The cost of transportation farther inland was too much to bear for many migrants; they ended up being subsidized by the Canadian government, much to the dismay of Governor General Elgin.

At the beginning of the shipping season one could count on making the 530-mile (850-km) trip from Québec to Toronto in about three days (continuous connection) for an adult fare of about 21 shillings 18 pence.[100] Otherwise, the trip could be made cheaply in open boats or barges, if one had up to twelve days to spare.[101] Even if one paid the rate, there was no guarantee of excellent service. One commentator in Toronto's *Globe* likened the overcrowding on the lake ships to conditions on board slave ships from Africa to the United States. In the Spring of 1847, dozens of passengers who had disembarked in Whitby, some 30 miles (50 km) east of Toronto, were forced to backtrack 12 miles (20 km) on foot in order to retrieve their baggage, which had been inadvertently deposited at Port Darlington.[102]

Steamship on Lachine rapids near Montréal

Credit: Library and Archives Canada 1982-145-57

By the time the Famine refugees had made their way to Lake Ontario in June 1847, they had already experienced more than their share of tragedy. Behind them they had left an unpredictable and unforgiving rural existence, marred by the repeated failure of their food staple, the potato. They had witnessed the destitution and death of loved ones, friends and neighbours who could not salvage enough food and were weakened and thus made vulnerable to disease. Ironically, the migrants had been the fortunate ones, because they had the means to leave their homeland—through funds raised personally or by remittances to leave Ireland and search for extended family and friends in North America. Etched in their memories was the trauma of having to leave their homes and the only life they had ever known. All that remained was the risk of venturing into the unknown and starting life anew in the interior of Canada.

The odyssey already marked by a sense of exile and compounded by the horrors of North Atlantic travel was still incomplete. In Toronto, they would soon encounter a host community frantically trying to cope with the mass migration and with the limits of contemporary medical science.

CHAPTER THREE

Toronto's "Great Calamity"

A S HUNDREDS OF IRISH famine refugees made their way from Kingston along the north shore of Lake Ontario, the question remains: did Upper Canadians anticipate the extent of the tragedy unfolding around them? Throughout 1846 and early 1847, it was clear that Torontonians knew of the tragic events unfolding in Ireland. On New Year's Day 1847, Charles Donlevy, editor of the Irish Catholic weekly *The Mirror*, offered a summary of the events of the past year. While Donlevy highlighted the blessings received by Canadians in Canada, his tone changed abruptly when recounting the cholera epidemic in India, the Mexican War, and the continued evil of American slavery as notable signposts of 1846. He saved his most bitter invective, however, for England: "In the bloody war of extermination waged against the unhappy people of Ireland, by the Sovereigns of England, millions were swept out of existence by starvation … Thousands perishing of want amidst surrounding plenty."[103]

Donlevy's *Mirror* had been Toronto's most effective window on the Famine, as the paper pumped out stories of depravation, starvation, and military intervention to protect Irish food stocks.[104] Catholics and Protestants in the city had responded to appeals for Irish aid throughout 1846 and early 1847, and it was generally known that the migration levels of the coming year would greatly exceed those of 1846.[105] There was some hope, however, that the potential influx of Irish workers would help with the expansion of Upper Canadian industry, where labour was in demand.[106]

In April, Toronto's citizens formed the Emigrant Settlement Association, which was intended "to put emigrants, on their arrival in the city, in the way of procuring steady employment, without delay." Members of the society, who paid an annual subscription of five shillings, were intent upon moving the emigrants quickly into the interior, where it was hoped that they could find employment as farm labourers in Toronto's rich agricultural hinterland. The Association also resolved to assist local mechanics and merchants in providing emigrant labour for their businesses and shops. Finally, the Association would also keep a registry of lands in order to provide emigrants with precise details about land available for sale or rent. One thing was clear, however. There would be no handouts: "as the Society merely contemplate affording advice, emigrants must not expect pecuniary assistance."[107] This attitude suggests that the colonials themselves were not unaware of the ideology espoused by Trevelyan and

Painting of King Street, Toronto, 1829

Credit: Library and Archives Canada, C-012703

others: that the poor must work for their daily bread, lest they become perpetually dependent on the generosity of the state or community.

One of the most acute observers of the Famine and its potential impact on Upper Canada was Michael Power, the first Roman Catholic bishop of Toronto, who was appointed in 1841 at the age of 37. Power's diocese stretched from Oshawa in the east to Fort William in the west, and from the shores of Lake Ontario and Lake Erie in the south, to the watershed of Lake Superior in the north. In January 1847, Power travelled to Europe to make his *ad limina* visit to Pope Pius IX in Rome, and to London, England, to address some problems in his diocese with the Colonial Secretary. During the British leg of his European tour, Power was overwhelmed by reports in the London newspapers about events in Ireland. On May 13, 1847, Power wrote to his flock indicating that the Pope urgently requested their prayers for Ireland "to implore the Father of Mercies to deliver the Irish Nation from the great calamity under which it is suffering." Hinting at the levels of Toronto's awareness of the Famine, he added,

> It is quite unnecessary that we should exhort you to respond to the Voice of the Vicar of Christ; for We know how intensely you feel for the sufferings of your Brethren in the Faith; and We have been informed that you have already contributed towards the alleviation of their distress with the greatest generosity.[108]

Two weeks after issuing the pastoral letter, he ventured to Ireland to recruit the Ladies of Loreto (Institute of the Blessed Virgin Mary) to his diocese, with the intention that they establish Catholic schools. While in Ireland, he saw the immediate effects of the Famine first hand; having completed his work in Ireland, he returned to Toronto via steamer just in time to see the migration as it took shape on the other side of the Atlantic. What he witnessed in Toronto merely revived the images of the tragedy to which he had already been exposed.

Toronto, the former provincial capital of Upper Canada, ceased to hold this civic honour in 1841, when the Union of the two provinces

Map of Upper Canada and Diocesan Divisions

came into being. Thereafter, the capital would alternate between the "old" provinces until the late 1850s, when the sleepy logging community of Ottawa was selected as the permanent seat of government, to the delight of no one outside of the new capital. Toronto's nearly 20,000 inhabitants lived along dirt (often muddy) thoroughfares in a broad band of wood-frame, brick, and stone houses between the Don River Valley to the east and Bathurst Street to the west. By 1847, only two roads in the city—King Street and Yonge Street—had been macadamized with gravel.[109] The southern extremity of the city was the bustling harbour on Lake Ontario; the northern limits of settlement were just beyond today's Queen Street (formerly Lot Street).

The harbour itself was naturally protected by a semi-circular peninsula that reached out into the bay from the east and then curved back towards the shore, providing a broad opening for vessels at the western end of the harbour. This western entrance was guarded by Fort York on the northern shore and by a lighthouse on the tip of the peninsula, named Gibraltar Point by John Graves Simcoe (1752–1806), the first lieutenant governor of Upper Canada. Known as the Toronto Islands today, this series of lightly wooded sandbars became an island only in 1858, when a storm swept away the narrow isthmus at its easternmost end, near the swampy flats at the mouth of the Don River.

The infrastructure that would help sustain the city as it was flooded by an influx of migrants numbering nearly twice the city's population between June and December 1847 involved several levels of government. The principal responsibility for immigration and regulations regarding transportation and health of the newcomers was the provincial government, which at that time was based in Montréal. The Provincial Secretary, the Hon. Dominick Daly, was the minister in charge of the immigration portfolio. Directly under him was the chief emigrant agent, Alexander C. Buchanan, whose office was in Quebec City, the first major port of entry for immigration to Canada.

Buchanan, although responsible for recording matters relating to migration and settlement, and reporting them directly to Daly and the British Colonial Office, was primarily concerned with these matters in Lower Canada (or Canada East, as it was officially called under the terms of the Union). Therefore, Buchanan was assisted by Anthony B. Hawke who, from his Kingston office, was responsible for migration and settlement for Upper Canada, as Buchanan was for Lower Canada. Given the size of the Upper province and the indisputable importance of Toronto as the region's major city, Hawke was served by Agent Edward McElderry, who maintained offices at Front and Yonge Streets in Toronto. Hawke did not know McElderry, who had been recommended to the department by Bishop Power and several other leading citizens. Speaking of his sub-agent, Hawke confessed, "He is no great scholar, but I have always found him zealous and correct."[110]

Hawke's agency was well aware that the migration of 1847 would be far greater than that of the previous year. In January, Hawke acknowledged to his superior, Buchanan, that there would be a "large migration," especially from Ireland. This did not seem to be terribly perplexing to Hawke who, like many other Upper Canadians, considered the increased levels of British and Irish migration to be necessary for a colony in need of agricultural and industrial labourers.

Officials conceded that there was a limit to the Crown Lands available in 1847, but that this situation might be remedied by the opening of the vast Huron Tract and the funnelling of migrants up the recently opened road between Garafraxa township and Owen Sound. Hawke estimated that Canada West could absorb "30 to 40 thousand of immigrants of the usual character during the current season." He confessed, however, that the "indigent" would be "scattered widely over the country" by his department.[111] Aware that disease might accompany the migrants from Ireland, given his experiences of the cholera epidemic of 1832, Hawke also had made arrangements that his sub-agents be secured in major Upper Canadian ports, and stationed a new agent at Cobourg.

In addition to creating his network of sub-agents, Hawke arranged contracts with the Royal Mail Line Steamship Company for transporting migrants from Kingston inland, and earnestly advised his subordinates to make certain that reception sheds were either constructed or improved in each port. Hawke was not shy about the fact he found Toronto "troublesome" and that he would be watching the situation there carefully.[112]

View of Toronto from the Jail, 1851

Perhaps it was the independence asserted by the Tory clique in Toronto that Hawke found so troublesome. At the municipal level of governance, the mayor of Toronto was the Hon. William Henry Boulton, who was supported by a network of friends and allies, some of whom were members of the City Council. His Council would be responsible for providing hospital and convalescent facilities under the auspices of a municipal Board of Health, which would receive part of its funding from the provincial government.

As early as February, City Council had formed the Board of Public Health after newspaper reports predicted that the sailing season might bring thousands from Ireland. The board was at first headed by Mayor Boulton, but he was later replaced by one of his allies, Alderman George Gurnett, himself a former mayor. The board's clerk, Constable Jonathan B. Townsend, was seconded from the local police force, as was his assistant, Constable William Foster. In time, the Emigrant Hospital and Convalescent Hospital would fall under the authority of the Board of Health. Given the complexity of the relationships between the levels of government and the personalities and egos therein, it appeared that managing the health, safety, and transport of Irish refugees in Toronto would be a Herculean operation.

The effectiveness of Toronto's reception of immigrants would depend on how well William Boulton kept his allies close to him while keeping his enemies at bay. Boulton was the son of D'Arcy Boulton, a scion of the conservative Family Compact, an oligarchy of like-minded landowners, churchmen, civic officials, professionals, and entrepreneurs—only some of whom had familial ties—who attempted to monopolize power in the Upper province until the late 1830s.

By the 1840s, remnants of the Compact and its allies still had a presence on the City Council in the likes of Boulton, George Gurnett, John Craig, Robert Beard, and John Ritchey, among others.[113] In January 1847, Boulton had only narrowly won his position as mayor, having survived a twelve-to-eleven vote by Council. The execution of the civic plan for efficient triage, treatment, and transportation of Irish refugees would hinge on the ability of Boulton's party to maintain control of the civic government. Closely tied to Boulton were Aldermen Hagarty and Gurnett, who would serve on the Board of Health, and Councillor John Ritchey, who would be instrumental in transforming the Toronto Hospital into an Emigrant Hospital. Ironically, this loose alliance of conservatives and Orangemen would be primarily responsible for the relief of the Famine migrants, most of whom would be Irish Catholics.

The procedure that was developed to process the thousands of expected migrants appeared reasonable enough in May. Once the migrants had cleared quarantine at Grosse Île and had made their way up the St. Lawrence to Montréal, it was expected that the remainder of the route would be taken by means of open sailing vessel or steamer to Kingston and other lake ports east of Toronto. Those who pressed on to Toronto would sail through the western end of the harbour and land at Dr. Rees's Wharf, at the foot of Simcoe Street (formerly Graves Street), near the site of what today is the Metropolitan Toronto Convention Centre.

There they would be assembled and separated into groups by McElderry, who would immediately send the healthy on their way to Hamilton or Niagara by boat, or enlist wagons and coaches to carry people farther inland. This approach would satisfy Hawke's policy of "scattering the indigent widely." Those who were overtly ill or who were showing the early symptoms of "ship's fever" or another contagion, or were in need of temporary food and shelter, would be housed in the sheds located at Rees's Wharf. McElderry was to be assisted by Constable Townsend (and, later, Constable Foster), who was required to keep the records of landings, the sick, and the dead for the Board of Health.

Sub-agent McElderry was making these plans as the first migrants began to arrive. They came not directly from Ireland, but from New York and Boston, two ports that were receiving migrants during the winter. By early May, steamers from Rochester carried a modest but steady stream of "American" Irish, which totalled 524 persons by mid-July.[114]

Credit: Library and Archives Canada C-001023

Entrance to Toronto

What appears clear in retrospect was that the Toronto operations, or for that matter the entire Emigrant Agency, began their preparations too late to be completely effective by May 1847. Although he has been accused of authoritarian and parsimonious behaviour by at least one historian,[115] Hawke was frantic to have operations in his region ready by late May. To this end, he instructed McElderry to repair the sheds as best he could. If the sheds could not be completed by this date, the sub-agent was to provide the indigent with "cheap lodgings" in the city. Moreover, Hawke instructed McElderry that, in the event that the sheds provided inadequate protection for the migrants in cold weather, McElderry was "at liberty to render them the usual assistance." Money was transmitted to McElderry to keep improving the sheds and, if needed, to hire a shed keeper to assist in their maintenance. It is true that Hawke rejected McElderry's petition to build an extension on the Toronto General Hospital, claiming it impractical, although the Chief Agent seized the opportunity to support the transfer of the Hospital for emigrant purposes, putting up £125 of public money in the process.[116]

While Hawke shared many of the laissez-faire assumptions of Trevelyan and others of his ilk—he rejected the idea of free passage for migrants, claiming that it would destroy the industriousness of Irish Canadian relatives who were sending remittances to finance many passages—he did not scrimp on the preparations to handle the influx of people in "Black '47," nor did he back away from arranging subsidized steamship passage for the indigent. If Hawke's plan was flawed, it was because the preparations were left too late and were committed in too hurried a fashion.[117]

When the first boatloads of migrants arrived from Lower Canada in June, the system faced its greatest test. As indicated earlier, the first ship-loads of Famine refugees began to arrive in Québec in mid-May (the first ship from an Irish port to arrive was the *Jane Black*, from Limerick, on May 23). By early June, the survivors were already steaming into Upper Canada. Many were showing signs of typhus, which, due to the nature of the disease, had been undetected at Grosse Île, Québec, or Montréal. On May 27, the Board of Health reported that, given the predicted influx of migrants and "the graat [sic] probability of contageous [sic] fever and other diseases injurious to the general health of the City," the City should make arrangements for the building of an Emigrant hospital on "the Peninsula opposite the City," to serve more effectively the emigrants while insulating the city from infection and disease. It was resolved that the sick would be kept in the sheds at Rees's Wharf and that the General Hospital at King and John Streets would not be used for any of the immigrants. Mr. McElderry would be offered funds to improve the existing sheds.[118]

Shortly after Toronto Council made its preparations, and just as the first waves of Irish refugees were venturing into Upper Canada, Provincial Secretary Dominick J. Daly issued instructions on behalf of Governor General Elgin. On June 7, municipal governments were ordered to establish "sheds and a hospital" in addition to appointing "Boards of Health of its own members, who shall draw up sanitary regulations to be observed by the emigrants receiving provisions of medical aid." The Board of Health was also required to "contract for the supply of bread and meat" and appoint an attending physician to administer to those immigrants consigned to the sheds and hospital. The Emigration agent would determine the daily provision of food and drink, beyond the required daily allotment of "3/4 lb. of bread and 3/4 lb. of meat for each adult, and 1/2 lb. of bread and 1/2 lb. of meat for each child." The relief period was to a maximum of six days.

To the satisfaction of Mayor Boulton and other councillors, the provincial government would cover the expenses, based on the weekly reports filed with the Provincial Secretary.[119] Under provincial mandate, the Board of Health became the principal means by which Toronto and other cities directed emigrant relief, although its funds were provided by the province and subject to provincial scrutiny through the office of the Emigrant Agent.

The landing of the sick and indigent was a harbinger of the future.

For the Toronto Board of Health, the directives had come none too soon. In the first week of June, the crush of Irish immigrants at Rees's Wharf was already straining the City's plan of action. On June 8, the *City of Toronto* dropped anchor at its namesake and proceeded to unload its human cargo of 700 adults and children, of whom 250 adults were described as "indigent," having arrived from Kingston at the "expense of the Government." Local journalists were quick to point out that these poorer migrants had come from the south and west of Ireland, whereas the remaining150 adults in "good circumstances" were described as having hailed from Northern Ireland and England.

This arrival was part of the continuing surge of Famine refugees inland; prior to June 7, at least 2,592 migrants had landed in Toronto, which turned out to be less than seven per cent of the season's total. This landing of the sick and indigent was a harbinger of the future. Subsequent landings of this type were equally chaotic, despite the often brutal efforts of port workers to keep the landings disciplined. John Young, a Scot travelling with his family on the steamer *Princess Royal*, likened the unloading at Toronto to the last roundup: "We got rid of most of our living cargo, whom they treated just like cattle driving them about, and tried to do the same with us, but we rebelled. They were all turned out and kept back with sticks till their luggage would be tumbled out after them."[120] Young was relieved when he was able to transfer to another steamer heading for Hamilton.

The Board of Health was soon under the firm hand of Alderman George Gurnett, who chaired his first meeting on June 14 and, on June 23, became its permanent chair. Gurnett and his associates on the Board—Charles Daly, Joseph Workman, MD, J.G. Beard, and Thomas J. Preston—would commence work in finding a hospital for the infected newcomers and would sharpen their plan of action to protect public health.[121] As they met, the local press was already warning of worse things to come as the statistical reports from Grosse Île and A.C. Buchanan's office were published.

On June 15, 1847, Torontonians learned that 40,000 migrants had set sail from Great Britain prior to May 19; Grosse Île was already feeling the strain of 1,150 sick in its hospitals and tents and 1,200 more sick on the ships that were lining up in the St. Lawrence. There were added reports of hundreds of deaths both at sea and on board the waiting ships. Citing the *Montreal Gazette*, Toronto's *British Colonist* printed, "We are not alarmists in this matter, but these figures show a fearful state of things … This is a most important matter for pestilence once let loose spares neither rich nor poor."[122] Toronto needed an emigrant hospital.

The question of a hospital for the incoming carriers of typhus, dysentery, and diarrhea had been hotly debated. In May, Mayor Boulton had requested that the military offer one of it barracks near Bathurst Street for this purpose; George Ryerson, the Quartermaster, refused the request, indicating that the local officers still wanted use of it. Nevertheless, Ryerson did not completely close the door on the idea, suggesting that, should the need arise, he would arrange the "erection of a temporary building on the hospital grounds."[123]

This news was hardly comforting, since the original plan for a new emigrant hospital, nicely isolated away from the city on the peninsula, was stalled. The Board of Health and the city had already indicated, in what was described by one physician as "magisterial language," that the General Hospital would not be used, although the hospital trustees were prepared to negotiate alternative arrangements.[124] At a meeting on

June 16, the Board of Health confirmed that the trustees of the General Hospital were prepared to rent "the Temple Chambers" on King Street and surrender the General Hospital at King and John Streets for use as the Emigrant Hospital.[125] The next day, the new hospital deal was accepted by the city and the trustees. The Board approached merchants Jacques & Hay for the provision of 50 sets of beds and bedding.[126]

Renamed the Emigrant Hospital, or, more colloquially, "the fever hospital," the building and its expansive grounds on the western edge of the city would become the exclusive preserve of the infected immigrants and their physicians and staff. The hospital itself was relatively new, having been constructed in 1819. After being used temporarily as the parliament of Upper Canada, it had reverted to its original purpose by 1829.[127]

Sketch of Emigrant Hospital

Credit: Toronto Public Library, J. Ross Robertson Collection, JRR 908

The second major initiative of the Board of Health was its drafting of specific regulations governing the behaviour of the immigrants and the local citizens. Here the Board was attempting to fulfill its dual mandate: first, to protect the citizens of Toronto from disease, and, second, to manage the health-care crisis that was deepening as each new day brought hundreds of new arrivals, mostly Irish, many of whom were stricken with illnesses of one sort or another.

The provisions for public safety were wide reaching: all emigrants were to be landed at Rees's Wharf, and any captain doing otherwise would face "penalties prescribed by city law"; all healthy immigrants were to be moved "by land or water" to their destinations by conveyance that "may" be provided by the emigrant agent; only the sick, or families of the sick, could occupy the sheds; immigrants remaining in the city would be prohibited from begging; tavern keepers and lodge-housekeepers were obliged to report any sign of sickness in their establishment to the High Bailiff of an officer at City Hall, with failure to do so possibly resulting in conviction under the law; and the Medical Officer was obliged to visit the sheds and any steamers or other vessels on a daily basis.[128]

Moreover, local residents were prohibited from housing any emigrants suspected of carrying disease. Cabs and carters were instructed not to transport any migrants into the city if they appeared ill.

In June, one casual observer, Mr. Larratt Smith, appeared rather impressed by Toronto's preparedness and the effective manner in which the city was treating the immigrants. Writing home to England, he reported,

> The City has passed some very stringent regulations with regard
> to Immigrants and measures are adopted to keep them as much
> as possible from being a nuisance to us. They arrive here to the
> extent of about 300 to 600 by any steamer. The sick are
> immediately sent to the hospital which has given up to them
> entirely and the healthy are fed and allowed to occupy the
> Immigrant sheds for 24 hours, at the expiration of this time,
> they are obliged to keep moving, their rations are stopped and
> if they are found begging, are imprisoned at once. Means of
> conveyance are provided by the Corporation to take them at
> once to the country ....[129]

Smith seemed to enjoy life in Toronto, despite the tragedy unfolding in the western wards of the city. These human "nuisances" neither inhibited him from marvelling at Toronto's gaslit streets, "handsome shops," or telegraph service, nor prohibited him from enjoying the social scene, the theatre, or taking excursions around Lake Ontario.[130] Perhaps as interesting as his observations of McElderry and Townsend doing their work is this young dandy's implicit praise of the idea that public relief was temporary; the newcomers ought to get to work or face the consequences.

By late June, the pattern was set for procedures at Rees's Wharf. McElderry, Townsend, and later Foster would meet the incoming ships: their first priority was to send the healthy migrants on their way—to Hamilton, the rural hinterlands around Toronto, or to London, or the neighbouring American states, via Niagara, if American border guards allowed it.[131]

Many Irish were able to re-establish ties with family and friends who had already settled in Canada over the previous 30 years. One must remember that the vast majority of the migrants, close to 85 per cent, left the Toronto area immediately, or departed the city after having recovered from illness.[132] Many of these migrants knew full well that there were friends and relations already living in Canada to assist them. In Limerick, for example, local newspapers had contained letters encouraging the region's farmers to join them in Canada.

In one such missive, Daniel McNamara exclaimed to his former neighbours in Limerick: "Thank God we have left that miserable country [Ireland] that we are in a good country now, and our children had good health. I have 3s 9d a day and steady work, laying out a new road and levelling hills."[133] Just to make his case stronger, McNamara added that another Limerick County man, Patrick Shine, "is doing well here," and that his daughters had good jobs in Toronto. While they did not record their names, or leave any visible mark upon the Toronto landscape, it must be conceded that for the majority of the Irish who entered the port of Toronto in 1847, their drama, after having landed, was played out while seeking their own Daniel McNamaras and Patrick Shines.

The sick were another matter. Four major difficulties manifested themselves in June and would remain problems for the duration of the sailing season. First, McElderry and others were struck by the sheer volume of migrants who had to be processed on a daily basis. Second, the Board of Health, overwhelmed by the huge volume of sick and indigent among the arrivals, began to suspect that officials in Kingston and Montréal were merely passing on their problems to Toronto. Third, it became clear that even with the new hospital facilities provided at King and John Streets, the medical urgency created by the numbers of sick and convalescent migrants was too much for the small facility to bear. Finally, the Board of Health had to deal with unprecedented numbers of dead and with the fear that typhus would spread throughout the city.

This latter problem was one that drew all citizens into the crisis, producing some moments of heroism and other incidents that the citizens of Toronto might wish to forget. By late autumn, Toronto had weathered the crisis, but barely. The events of the season had illustrated how underprepared the city had been. If not for the accident of geography— Toronto being so far inland—the results of the "summer of sorrow" as it came to be called could have been far worse.

The first major problem was handling the sheer volume of people arriving in Toronto. Between the arrival of the *City of Toronto* on June 7, and over the next sixteen days, an additional 4,608 migrants, mostly Irish, landed at Rees's Wharf, an average of over 300 migrants per day. The aggregate numbers and the daily numbers continued to rise as the summer wore on. In the eight days between August 2 and August 10, 3,650 migrants arrived, at an average of over 450 per day.[134] Of course, these are averages; some days may have witnessed only several hundred, while other days could have been likened to the arrival, earlier in the month, of the steamship bearing the city's name.

By the end of the year, Constable J.B. Townsend reported that 38,560 migrants (over 75 per cent of whom were Irish)[135] had entered the port of Toronto between May and December. Of that tally, 35,630 had moved right through to other places, presumably Upper Canada and the United States, when allowed.[136] Townsend indicated that 1,124 had died in Toronto, either in the hospital or in lodgings in the city. When he issued his report in February 1848, he observed that 781 migrants remained in private lodgings in Toronto, while 623 were still inmates in either the Emigrant Hospital or the Convalescent Hospital, and 89 were occupants of the Widows and Orphans Refuge.[137]

The Board of Health could be commended for being able to process so large a number of persons in such a short period of time. Only 4,355 of these migrants, approximately 11.3 per cent, had to be triaged to one of several medical facilities operated by the Board of Health.

Reflecting in a scholarly manner upon the statistics, with the advantage of hindsight, in our own time is a very different reality from actually living with the pressure of triaging hundreds of immigrants per day, with a small staff and a far less developed understanding of microbiology and epidemiology. Naturally, in the Toronto of 1847, health workers and the Emigration Agent were deeply concerned by the large numbers of sick and indigent people landing at Rees's Wharf. Early in the season, one local wag had already referred to Toronto colourfully as "a general Lazaretto"—another name for a leper hospital. The arrivals that Townsend described to the Board on August 18 seemed to embody all the elements of the crisis faced both dockside and at the corner of King and John. According to Townsend's minutes,

The Board of Health had to deal with unprecedented numbers of dead and with the fear that typhus would spread throughout the city.

> Emigrants arrived from Kingston yesterday, 700. Several of them were in the last stage of sickness, and died shortly after reaching the Hospital. The sheds were reported full, but as clean as circumstances will permit. The Emigrant Agent [McElderry] reports that 1000 emigrants left Kingston, but 300 of them arrived at Whitby and other places, on the way up. Of the 700 that came to Toronto, 30 paid their own expenses. The greater number were forwarded to the country yesterday, and the remainder would be sent this morning.[138]

The numbers had grown to such a degree at the Hospital that the dining rooms had to be converted into hospital rooms and the wood-shed had to substitute for the dining hall.[139] Ironically, McElderry could recall that, earlier in April, he had asked Hawke for funds to construct an addition to the hospital; Hawke had refused, claiming that the sums paid per immigrant, one shilling per person per day, were "considerable" and reasonable, based on the precedent of the cholera epidemic of 1832.[140]

Nevertheless, the events of these few summer days underscored the troubles affecting the care given to emigrants in Toronto: too many were coming and there were too few facilities to house them.

For Toronto and other municipalities, the costs of medical treatment and food had become staggering. By July, Hawke was under siege from his agents for requests for more money. In 1846, his agency had expended only £2,000 in salaries in expenses; by mid-July, Toronto alone would be in need of over £915, with Hamilton, Cobourg, and Bytown collectively needing a total exceeding £838.[141] By season's end, medical costs in Toronto, including medicines, food, and furniture and excluding salaries, soared to close to £5,200; and the estimated costs in the entire region of Canada West had inflated to £35,635, a sum that included salaries, food, and transportation subsidies.[142]

If Hawke had a streak of Scrooge in him, or had the very least fiscal caution, it was for good reason. The expenses of dealing with the numbers of sick and indigent migrants were out of control. He confided to Buchanan, "The expenditure is indeed tremendous. But it cannot be avoided—not an unnecessary shilling is expended that I am aware of ...."[143]

Toronto was sharing part of the burden with other municipalities along the shores of the Home and Newcastle Districts (currently the Regional Municipality of Durham and Northumberland County). Most migrants were too poor to pay for their passage out of Montréal, suggesting that even if these Irish Famine migrants had sufficient means to cross the ocean, their resources were quickly exhausted once they were faced with food, accommodation, medical, and transportation charges in Canada. Finally, too many were coming in advanced states of illness, suggesting either duplicity further down the lake or in other towns, or the earnest desire of the migrants themselves to avoid detection in the eastern part of the province.

Members of Toronto's Board of Health and the public scribes began to wonder if agents and physicians in the ports of call farther to the east were doing their jobs properly. The case of Mary Brennan, for example, raised suspicions that doctors in Kingston were merely passing on their tougher cases for their colleagues in Toronto.

On August 26, John Townsend reported to the Board of Health that, on the previous day, he had discovered a seven-year-old girl, Mary Brennan, with a broken thigh at Rees's Wharf. She had travelled from Ireland with her grandmother, whom Townsend described as a "feeble old woman" in the early stages of fever.[144] The pair had journeyed as far as Kingston, where Mary was run over by a cart. According to the grandmother, the attending surgeon at the Kingston General Hospital set the bone and indicated that young Mary would be fine as far as Toronto and that the child was refused permission to remain in Kingston. Later, officials in Kingston protested that the grandmother, counter to the doctor's orders, had absconded with the child and boarded the steamer to Toronto, where they were to stay with friends.[145]

While the "counter" story exonerated the Kingston physician, it also exposed the poor supervision offered in Kingston, if patients could flee the hospital and proceed upriver, whether physicians wanted them to or not. Issues of culpability aside, on September 5, Mary Brennan died at the Convalescent Hospital. Her grandmother, Mary Tobin, described as a Catholic widow, was admitted to the same institution and released eight days after her granddaughter's death.[146]

The Brennan case also raised questions about the quality of transportation between Montréal and Toronto. In July, A.B. Hawke complained that too many emigrants were falling ill between Montréal and Kingston, largely due to the length of time—five days—it took open barges to transport passengers. Because the barges were open, migrants were also susceptible to "variable weather," which weakened their condition significantly. Hawke made arrangements that more passengers be taken by steamship, which would shorten the journey by about three days.[147]

In retrospect, this action taken by Hawke in the early summer seems rather disingenuous. As early as April, he had made arrangements that the Royal Mail Line, which operated steamships (with barges in tow) to all major Canadian ports on Lake Ontario, would have a monopoly on government-assisted emigrant travel. An "indigent emigrant" wishing to travel from Kingston to Cobourg would be subsidized at a rate of 4 shillings; passage from Kingston to Whitby and Toronto was set at 6 shillings and 3 pence.[148] Hawke had even anticipated the fast dispersal of indigent passengers at Toronto. The government would subsidize travel from Toronto to Niagara, Queenston, and Hamilton at a rate of 2 shillings and 6 pence per person. These subsidies were approximately one third less the cost of a regular fare.[149]

If Hawke had made such arrangements, the question remains why so many passengers used less efficient and longer forms of transportation, at such a high human cost. One suspects that it was far cheaper for the government to subsidize the cost of barges and sailing craft or that the Royal Mail Line, in an effort to maximize its profits, attached more barges to steamships than even Hawke had anticipated.

More effective forms of travel, however, did not necessarily increase the chances of healthier immigrants arriving at Toronto. In August, the *Globe* reprinted a story from the *Streetsville Review* that offered a scathing evaluation of conditions on board some of the steamships:

> We are informed by a gentleman who came up by one of the steamers from Kingston to Toronto the other day that the manner in which the emigrant passengers were packed was truly shocking. The poor creatures, he tells us, were crowded together like herrings in a barrel, and many had difficulty gasping for a breath of fresh air. Our informant (who was from the other side of the lake) remarked that the condition of the unfortunate live cargo reminded him of the accounts which he had read of the stowage of Negroes on a slave ship ... Why, the hardships undergone in circumstances like the above, would be sufficient to produce an attack of typhus even in the subject who landed in Canada comparatively healthy and robust. On Lake Ontario the heat at present is often as great as a tropical

climate, and its effects upon persons unseasoned to its glow, and crowded together like sheep in a fold, may be readily imagined.[150]

While one might quibble with the technicalities of the medical diagnosis offered by the author, the observations implicate the Royal Mail Line Company for gross negligence in transporting the migrants. Such behaviour was confirmed when it was reported to the *Globe* that migrants landed in Cobourg drenched and not given shelter, and 130 Scots were dumped in the same port, even though their destination was Whitby, an action the paper condemned as "highly disgraceful and [deserving] of the reprobation of the press throughout the Province."[151] John Young, while on board the *Princess Royal*, which sailed from Kingston to Toronto, commented that his father complained to an unsympathetic captain about the number of Irish migrants, many of whom were sick "and so many were packed in that we had not room to stir."[152]

"… so many were packed in that we had not room to stir."

Stephen De Vere, who had exposed the trans-Atlantic ships as the virtual "coffin ships" of popular historical memory, was even more outraged by the steamship system as it operated in Canada West. In his lengthy exposé to the Colonial Secretary, Earl Grey, at the end of the shipping season, De Vere had been critical of the immigration process from the ports of departure to the wharves of Lake Ontario. Despite all that he had seen and experienced, including Grosse Île, he saved his most bitter invective for the Canadian government's handling of steamship travel from Montréal to Toronto. He was appalled that the government had entered into a monopolistic venture with a single steamship company, without having made provisions for how passenger travel would be regulated. Without such safeguards for the health and safety of immigrants, De Vere observed,

I have seen incommodious, and ill ventilated Steamers arriving at the Quay in Toronto after 48 hour's [sic] passage from Montréal freighted with foetid cargoes of 11 & 1200 Government Emigrants, of all ages and Sexes, the healthy who had just arrived from Europe mixed with the half recovered convalescents of the Hospitals,

unable during that time to lie down, almost to sit—In almost
every boat were clearly marked cases of actual fever—the dead
and living huddled together—sometimes the crowds were stowed
in open barges, and towed after the steamer, standing like Pigs
upon the Deck of a Cork and Bristol Packet. A poor woman died
in the Hospital here [Toronto] in the consequence of having been
trodden down when weak, and fainting; in one of the Barges.
I have myself accompanied the Emigrant Agent [McElderry]
on his visit of Duty to inspect the Steamer on her arrival, seen
him stagger back like one struck, when first meeting a current
of foetid infection exhaled from between her decks.[153]

De Vere praised McElderry's "indefatigable" efforts, but concluded
that the Lake Ontario steamships were the primary cause of the spread
of fever throughout the province.

Daily increases in the numbers of sick being transferred from the
wharf to King and John Streets meant that the Emigrant Hospital was
overloaded. Reports in the early summer indicated that the wards, hall-
ways, and verandas of the building were stuffed with the sick and dying.

In June, the Board of Health had hired Dr. George Grasett as the
chief attending surgeon of the facility.[154] A resident steward and his wife
lived in the lower levels of the hospital, and a nursing staff and orderlies
did the bulk of the work on the wards. Grasett had a staff of orderlies
who were paid £3 per month, a chief orderly who was paid 15
shillings more, and female nurses who made a paltry £1 and 15 shillings,
5 shillings less than the hospital's washer woman.[155] Each attending
physician required two nurses; the patient-to-nurse ratio had been set
at 70 to one.[156]

As early as mid-June, it became clear that the hospital was too small
and required special holding areas. Moreover, it became increasingly
obvious that the sheds on Rees's Wharf had been found wanting in
almost every way. As a result, the Board of Health contracted the building
of sheds on the grounds of the hospital, initially 50 by 10 feet (15 m
by 3 m), open-sided, with two rows of seats "to protect the emigrants

therein from the suns rays." In June and July, tenders were advertised for the building of more sheds; by August there were close to 700 patients in the Emigrant Hospital and still others housed in sixteen sheds, most of which exceeded the original sheds in size (75 feet [22 m] by 20 feet [6 m]).[157] An interesting feature of the tendering process for the sheds was that the contract was won by Councillor John Ritchey, a close political ally of both Mayor Boulton and Alderman Gurnett, chair of the Board of Health. Ritchey secured £250 each for the sheds his men constructed.

Controversy swirled about the hospital. Constable J.B. Townsend was responsible for the management of people in the sheds on the hospital grounds. In the sheds, doctors and nurses attended to the Irish migrants, who, on pleasant days, were reported to have lain upon the lawns of the facility in the open air. Townsend was responsible for recording the daily numbers of patients in the hospital and in the sheds. According to Dominick Daly's instructions in June, these would be the figures upon which the six shilling per diem per patient (a notable increase since April) would be based. In early August, a local newspaper did a count of the Irish in the facilities and discovered that the numbers had been overstated by Townsend by close to 300. The local press queried: had the operators of the hospital inflated the numbers of sick in order to maximize the government's per diem?

Townsend quickly tried to explain away the discrepancy by saying that patients often left the hospital grounds without detection, and that it was very difficult to keep track of their comings and goings, given the sheer volume of numbers on the site. For the sake of greater transparency, and perhaps to deflect any further controversy surrounding his work, Townsend, as the Clerk of the Board, published weekly hospital statistics in the Toronto newspapers. The public remained leery of what was actually happening at the site.

The hospital did not need this negative publicity or any other controversy given the confusion surrounding the delivery of patient care during the summer. It had already experienced a shocking loss when, on July 16, George Grasett, the chief medical officer at the Emigrant

Hospital, died of fever. He was buried from his brother's home the following day.[158]

That same month, Ritchey's construction workers, who had been building the new sheds on the grounds of the hospital, lay down their tools, refusing to continue, because several of their number had fallen ill. Grasett's colleagues squabbled among themselves over the issue of who would succeed him and how to treat typhus victims effectively. One of his successors, Dr. Reginald Henwood also became ill, leaving the administration of the hospital to John Ludgate, the dispenser of the hospital's pharmacy, in charge of the operation until August 26, when the new resident medical officer, Dr. Alex McDougall, arrived on the scene.

This transition of power was made more precarious by the fact that hospital workers were in the middle of a wage dispute, claiming that Montréal hospital workers were better paid. This indignity, they claimed, was made much worse by the fact that many of their colleagues had become ill and some had died while discharging their duties.[159] One these workers, head nurse Susan Bailey, died shortly before the end of August. She was only 32.[160]

Particularly disconcerting was the public debate over the methods being used to treat patients in the hospital. Through Grasett's last days and during the ensuing scramble to secure additional medical help, the Board of Health was hampered by public exchanges that cast doubt on the medical operations at King and John. On July 13, while Grasett was gravely ill, and in the wake of Dr. O'Brien's resignation, the Board of Health hired Dr. John B. Rankin; almost immediately, problems arose between the new attending physician and the Board. Within three days, Rankin had resigned his post, having openly disagreed with the Board. While the Board's friends at Hugh Scobie's *British Colonist* alleged that this episode was little more than Rankin's vanity in not having been appointed "chief" medical officer,[161] there may have been some substance behind Rankin's allegations.

Rankin had questioned the hospital's being located in town, suggesting in an open letter to the *British Colonist* dated August 26, 1847, that the sick should have been transported to an area outside of

Toronto. Having concluded that the fever seemed to be transmitted by lice, he was adamant that sanitation measures be improved when caring for patients. He was also puzzled about why chlorine had not been used as a disinfectant.

Given the rather rudimentary manner in which fevers were treated in the 1840s, and the fact that most admissions to hospital were on the grounds of having a fever (27.7 per cent of patients between 1847 and 1855),[162] one can understand Rankin's concern that the most effective means of preventing the spread of the disease be put into effect in Toronto's main medical facility. In fact, the provincial government had contracted several scientists to come up with an appropriate disinfectant for ships and barges, with only modest results.[163] However, with the hospital's dirty laundry literally flapping in the winds of the free press, the Board of Health appointed Dr. Joseph Hamilton to join Dr. Derry and Dr. Reginald Henwood and Dr. Edwin Henwood to the hospital.[164] Sadly, in November, Hamilton would die of complications derived from the fever that he had contracted in the course of his work.[165]

Rumours also began to circulate that hospital workers were drinking or reselling the wine supplies that were intended to help restore health to the fever victims. In early August, a correspondent to the *Mirror* reported that the use of wine and brandy to help treat the fever victims was ineffective because the doses being administered were too small.[166] On the contrary, wrote another correspondent under the pseudonym "Medicus," the problem was rooted in the fact that too many spirits were being administered at the hospital. While the paper made little of this treatment at the time, the writers did draw upon it when they unleashed a barrage of criticism at hospital managers in September. At that time, Donlevy's paper suggested that given the problems in counting the inmates on the grounds at King and John, and given the regular supply of alcohol to the premises: "About two thousand gallons of wine and brandy have been drunk to the health of the patients, not forgetting absent friends." In the process, the *Mirror* suggested that the Irish patients were not getting the best possible treatment.[167]

With the city gripped in near panic as a result of the constant flow of immigrants into the port and the resultant stream of carts and hearses carrying the most unfortunate of these to the city's burial grounds, the mayor called a public meeting. On Friday, July 16, 1847, at the old City Hall, local Catholic businessman Michael P. Hayes chaired a meeting of Toronto's notables, including Anglican Bishop John Strachan; the Chief Justice of the Province, William A. Baldwin; George Gurnett; Edward McElderry; E.H. McSherry; and Hugh Scobie; among others. It was an impressive gathering of Roman Catholics and Protestants, Reformers and Tories, clergy, laity, and medical officials, all of whom shared one thing in common: their concern for the human tragedy unfolding rapidly around them. The principal task of the gathering was to rethink the use of hospital space in the city, given the huge numbers of those in need and the limited space and funds available in Toronto.

The meeting made five resolutions, the first three of which promised significant changes to the manner in which medical and financial relief was administered. First, the meeting resolved that since the convalescents were "too weak to earn subsistence," they ought to be cared for in a separate convalescent hospital. In addition, it was decided that provision should be made for shelter for destitute widows and orphans. Second, on a motion made by William Baldwin and John Cameron, the city would petition for the balance of the Irish Relief Fund that had been raised locally. This motion acknowledged, in a public way, that the Famine was no longer just an Irish problem, but a Canadian one as well. Third, the meeting struck a relief committee to continue collecting private subscriptions for local relief. The ten-person committee was an interesting mix of Board of Health officials (Gurnett), two physicians, and several local politicians. Most significant, however, for a city that would garner a reputation for sectarian bigotry and violence, several Catholics were appointed to the committee, indicating that when so many lives were at stake, there was no room for sectarian prejudice.[168]

By August, the Board of Health, in keeping with the resolutions of the July 16 meeting, managed to relieve the situation at King and John Streets with the creation of two temporary institutions: the Convalescent

Hospital and the House of Refuge for Widows and Orphans. Grasett's successors were concerned about placing the recovering patients too close to those in the worst phases of disease; similarly, there was concern about releasing those in recovery, lest there be panic within the local population that the typhus virus would spread in epidemic proportions. In August, the Board of Health rented, from John Henry Dunn, a brick building at the corner of Front and Bathurst Streets.

Dunn's property would serve as a Convalescent Hospital, to which patients in recovery at the Emigrant Hospital could be moved. The erection of this new facility provided the convalescing patient with a healthier environment for recovery and offered a more efficient use of space in the "fever hospital." Shortly after opening, the Convalescent Hospital would house over 300 patients daily. From there, patients would either be released to continue their trek into the interior, be sent back to the Emigrant Hospital should they suffer a relapse (usually bad cases of diarrhea), or, if they were widows and orphans, sent to the House of Refuge, a former barracks at Bathurst and Queen Streets. This latter facility had been finally made available by the military for public use.

For those Irish who did not survive to see either of these convalescent institutions, there were serious questions about how the city was going to dispose of their bodies. The Board of Health regulations regarding the burial of the dead had been quite explicit. Bodies were sent to the "dead house" at the Emigrant hospital. There, the orderly of the dead house recorded their names and the bodies were prepared for burial. Each would have a wooden coffin. Thomas Ryan had been awarded the contract for burying the Catholic dead, while H.B. Williams was commissioned to handle the arrangements for Protestants and Anglicans. Each undertaker would transport the bodies to their respective denominational cemetery: St. Paul's Roman Catholic burial ground, which lay adjacent to the church of the same name, south of Queen Street and east of Power Street, or St. James Cemetery for Anglicans and Protestants. H.B. Williams had the additional task of transporting the dead with unknown religious affiliations or lack of kin to the potter's field adjacent to St. James Cemetery.

Shortly after opening, the Convalescent Hospital would house over 300 patients daily.

Once the bodies had arrived at their resting place, the Board of Health mandated that the graves be dug to a depth allowing for three feet of earth between the top of the coffin and the level ground, and then that the earth be heaped to a level of at least one foot above the ground.[169] Given the number of corpses to be buried on a daily basis, in some cases deep trenches would have been dug to accommodate the volume; however, it would be erroneous to assume (as does popular mythology) that the bodies of the Famine Irish were dumped into mass graves. Such disrespect would have raised public ire, violated Board of Health regulations, and angered Bishop Power, who had a track record of being meticulous about how Catholics (about 70 per cent of the dead) were buried.[170] By year's end, 1,124 migrants had died—863 at the hospital—and had been buried in Toronto.[171]

Few of these migrant families left their stories for posterity. One particularly gripping exception is the story of the Willis family of Limerick. Both parents and five children boarded the *Jessie* at Limerick with 482 other passengers on April 18, 1847. Before the ship sailed, one son fell ill and had to be left in Limerick. After departing Ireland, the ship spent 56 days on the Atlantic, during which time 26 people died, including the Willis's eighteen-year old son and ten-year-old

Credit: Edward Kelly, *The Story of St. Paul's Parish*, 1922

Photo of Old St. Paul's

daughter, Martha. When the ship arrived at Grosse Île in June, spending thirteen days in quarantine, another daughter, Mary, age seventeen, was removed to the lazarettos (hospital sheds) of the island, where she later died. The remaining three members of the Willis family landed at Québec on June 26, proceeding to Toronto, where they were quickly dispatched inland.[172] They ventured by road to Brantford, in the London District, where both the father and the remaining son died of fever, leaving only the mother under the watchful eye of the local Anglican priest, the Reverend James Campbell Usher.[173]

Stories like those of the Willis family were common, although the names of many have been lost because of the hasty way that names were recorded during the crisis and due to the loss of records over the past century and a half. Stories of the more famous victims, such as Dr. George Grasett, Bishop Michael Power, and Edward McElderry have been preserved.

The burial of the dead was not without controversy. There had been complaints in the past about the stench that came from the hearses, either en route to the burial ground or when they were dispatched to their livery. The events of August 14, however, scandalized "Toronto the Good." In a bizarre episode, a hearse being driven by an employee of Thomas Ryan, the Catholic undertaker, broke down after hitting a rut on King Street en route to St. Paul's Cemetery. Four coffins tumbled off the wagon and smashed in the middle of the thoroughfare. Onlookers were horrified when two "nearly, if not quite naked" bodies spilled out of what was, by law, supposed to be a casket built for a single corpse! The four caskets had housed five bodies.[174] The *Mirror* quickly jumped on the story and accused public health officials of impropriety and scandalous practices:

> It was quite manifest from the tenour [sic] of their strictures
> [the press], that had the proprietor been of a different religious
> denomination, very little would have been said about the matter …
> One would almost have imagined that Ryan's Hearse was the
> white horse of the Book of Revelation and the driver was a death's
> head and cross bones. Two bodies had been found in one coffin.

Mirabile dictu. But who put the bodies there? The most searching inquiry failed to identify Mr. Ryan as any participant in the act. Well, what has since come to light? Why, just this—nearly three hundred patients less in the hospital than Mr. Toby Townsend's daily bulletins have recorded and Mr. Const Townsend in his cab every morning visited the hospital … No doubt counted beds, but forgot to search for bodies.[175]

The case went to court but was dismissed for lack of evidence, but the mystery of the episode still remains: who was responsible for this macabre violation of the law? Ryan, as undertaker, would have had to pay 10 shillings per interment at St. Paul's, which suggests that perhaps Ryan had packed two bodies into one coffin to save burial costs.[176] But since Ryan would have included this charge in his fee, and the dead house orderlies would have supervised the transfer of the bodies, cost-saving is an unlikely motive.

It is possible that hospital staff was shortchanging Ryan by underestimating the number of coffins released, which would ultimately allow the hospital to retain the government's per diem for a person who was actually dead, but not recorded as such. As the *Mirror* indicated, the body counts at the hospital could be inaccurate. Perhaps Ryan and some staff members worked together for personal financial gain. Whether the orderlies or Ryan's workers were culpable or not, public confidence in the management of the Emigrant Hospital was shaken.

Even when the dead were recorded and buried routinely, without controversy, there was still a sense among some civic workers that Toronto was witnessing only the first chapter in what might prove to be a very long winter for the undertakers. As early as August, Constable Townsend reported that he feared that despite the effective triage at the wharf that directed healthy migrants to the countryside, the Board of Health might not have seen the last of them.

A boomerang effect was beginning to appear. Those who had been sent off "healthy" by McElderry were now returning to Toronto on foot, sick. "The sheds are full, and Emigrants laying about in all directions," reported Townsend. "A considerable portion of the emigrants sent to the Hospital yesterday were parties who had been previously sent into the country, apparently healthy … but a few days work had completely overcome them, and they were accordingly sent back …."[177]

Later that month, M.B. Davis was so convinced of the impending problems with streets full of the poor and beggars "with the Canadian winter … yet to be encountered," he urged Mayor Boulton to raise government funds to employ healthy migrants in the macadamization of the Toronto streets or in building a railway from Toronto to Weston. The wages from these projects would allow them to purchase food and rent shelter and save them from "what misery is yet in store for them."[178]

Although Toronto's City Council and medical officers had put an immigrant reception and health action plan in place by June 1847, it became evident fairly quickly that the city and its aid workers and politicians were completely overwhelmed. The contemporary medical treatment for typhus was ineffective; hospital facilities did not have adequate room for all the sick; generally, doctors and the police did a poor job of monitoring the comings and goings of the migrants after their initial triage as "healthy" at the wharf and those in hospital; and, among the medical staff, egos clashed about the best treatment of "fever."

Perhaps the most horrific perception of the summer's events was the suspicion that some aid workers and politicians might be using the immigrant crisis as a means of lining their own pockets. Despite all adversity, however, civic leaders rarely hesitated to review policies and practices when they were found wanting, and made valiant efforts—albeit ad hoc efforts, at times—to calm the mayhem that swirled all around them. Whether inspired by fear, desperation, or altruism, Toronto's leaders and the general citizenry were called to address the "Irish" crisis in a meaningful way. In retrospect, it may have been the city's greatest emergency since the Americans looted and burned the town, then called York, during the War of 1812.

CHAPTER FOUR

Making Sacrifices and Pointing Fingers: Citizens Respond

LATER IN THE NINETEENTH CENTURY, Toronto would become known as the "city of churches," with hundreds of buildings providing sacred space for all of Christianity's principal denominations. In the 1840s, there was neither a large number of churches in Toronto nor a diversity of denominations. In 1848, the population of the city was 23,503. Of that figure, about 25 per cent (5,903) were Roman Catholic; the rest belonged to the Anglican or mainstream Protestant denominations: Presbyterian (both Church of Scotland and dissenters), Baptist, and Methodist (both Wesleyan and Primitive).[179]

While congregations had met in private homes during the city's early history, formal stone and brick church structures began to appear in the early 1800s. The Anglicans dominated both the numbers of Protestants and the architectural skyline of the city with their impressive St. James Cathedral, on King Street East. Originally a small wooden chapel built in 1803, the Anglican nerve centre of the city was gutted by fire and rebuilt of stone in Gothic style in 1832.[180] From his rectory at St. James, Anglican bishop John Strachan oversaw a population of 11,577 souls (an 1851 estimate) in Toronto,[181] and thousands more spread from the Newcastle District in the east, from Peterborough to Georgian Bay in the north, and from Peel County to the Gore District at the head of Lake Ontario. The military had its own Anglican chapel, St. John the Evangelist, in the west end of the city near Fort York at what is now Victoria Square.[182]

Other denominations had a strong visible presence in the city as well. In 1822, Roman Catholics had built St. Paul's Church at what are now Queen and Power Streets. From the time of his arrival in June 1842, Bishop Michael Power used the modest brick church as his Cathedral. Construction of the massive St. Michael's Cathedral closer to the centre of the city at Bond and Shuter Streets, began in 1845 and would be consecrated in 1848, less than a year after Power's death. In 1818, Toronto's many Wesleyan Methodists had built a small wooden chapel for worship near the corner of King and Jordan Streets. The Primitive Methodists constructed a 600-seat red brick chapel in 1832.[183] Finally, by 1834, the Presbyterians had built St. Andrew's Church at Adelaide and Church Streets, the first formal place of worship in Toronto for their denomination.[184]

The Famine moment brought to Toronto a disproportionate number of Roman Catholics into what had essentially been a colonial Protestant town. Prior to the Famine period, the vast majority of Irish immigrants to Upper Canada had been Protestant at a ratio of about two Protestants for every Catholic. Irish ports such as Cork, Derry, Belfast, and Dublin transported Protestant migrants from both the predominantly Protestant province of Ulster and from the pockets of Irish Protestants in such counties as Cork, Tipperary, and Wexford.[185]

The peak year of 1847 tipped the religious balance in Toronto substantially in favour of Irish Catholics, who hailed from nearly all of the counties in distress. The high proportion of Catholics among the 38,560 migrants to Toronto is confirmed by both the records of deaths in the city in 1847, and by the meticulous ledger kept at the Convalescent Hospital. Of the dead, nearly 70 per cent, or 757 persons, were interred in the Roman Catholic cemetery, a figure that suggests that the ratio between Catholic and Protestant migrants for 1847 was the reverse of what it had been previously, with Catholics now dominant. This observation is substantiated by those patients who survived the sickness. Of the 2,030 inmates in the Convalescent Hospital for whom "religion" was recorded, 85.9 per cent (1,744) were listed as Roman Catholic.[186]

While it could be argued that the Roman Catholics, because of their socio-economic status in Ireland, may have been more vulnerable to illness, the sheer numbers of Catholics indicates that they were a significant portion of the 1847 migration. Commentaries from Grosse Île, emigration agents, and churchmen confirm this numerical dominance of Irish Catholics.

Given the obvious numbers of Catholics in the wards of the Emigrant and Convalescent hospitals, in addition to the sixteen sheds that had been built at King and John Streets by the end of August,[187] Roman Catholic clergy were conspicuous in their presence among the migrants.[188] Working out of St. Paul's Church and the new Episcopal Palace, which had just been completed next to the shell of St. Michael's Cathedral (now Church and Shuter Streets), Bishop Power could count on the assistance of three priests: John O'Reilly, Thaddeus Kirwin, and J.J. Hay.

Power also enlisted the gifted Jean-Baptiste Proulx, a former missionary. Proulx was responsible for ministering to all Catholics within a 50-mile (80-km) radius of Toronto. Proulx would encounter the Irish "inland" in Whitby, Highland Creek, Newmarket, Toronto Gore, Port Credit, and Oakville.[189] O'Reilly and Kirwin were 30 and 31 years of age respectively; each had been ordained only for one year. Hay, at 29, was the veteran, having been ordained five years and having served as secretary to Bishop Power for much of that time.[190]

All three men were Canadian-born of Irish parents; each served their countrymen in a variety of ways. Every day would require them to visit the sheds and Emigrant Hospital, where they would offer comfort to the sick, hear confessions, and anoint the dying with the sacrament of Extreme Unction (colloquially termed "the last rites"). They would also be required to be present to say prayers and offer solace to loved ones at the final committal of the dead in the Catholic burial ground, immediately adjacent to St. Paul's Church. (For more information on the burial ground, see Appendix D.) These efforts required sturdy legs

The peak year of 1847 tipped the religious balance in Toronto substantially in favour of Irish Catholics ....

for cross-town walks, a strong stomach to face the misery that awaited them at King and John Streets, and robust health to avoid contracting the "fever" from those to whom they ministered.

By the last week of August, however, these priests had run out of luck. Local papers reported that all three had contracted typhus and were being treated at the Episcopal Palace. Worse still, Father Jeremiah Ryan, who had been called in to replace O'Reilly, became ill shortly after his arrival, leaving the countryside in the hands of Proulx and the city with only Bishop Power himself visiting the sheds and burying the dead.[191] Power was virtually alone in his ministry to the Irish until the arrival of veteran priest John Carroll. Carroll would take over temporarily for Kirwin, whom Power had dispatched to Niagara to convalesce.[192]

When Sister Teresa Dease IBVM and four other members of the Loretto Sisters arrived at Power's door on September 16, Dease described the countenance of the bishop as one of shock, fatigue, and worry. Power warned them that there was "plague raging in the house"; at supper that evening, he was extra cautious, examining closely everything that the sisters were about to consume. His principal fear was that this highly sought after group of women, who were to be the backbone of Catholic education in the city, might become infected by the same sickness that had felled all of his priests. According to Dease, the demeanor of the bishop and the frail Father Hay seemed to mimic the dour and Spartan appearance of Power's home, which she described as looking "bare and oppressively lonely … an abode on which the sun of this world's prosperity had never shone."[193]

Her observations were not far off the mark. It was highly likely that Power, now thoroughly exhausted, had already been exposed to the *rickettsia* bacteria that caused typhus, or was weak to the point that any exposure to the contagion might be fatal to him.

On September 22, within a week of the arrival of the Lorettos, Power had begun to display the first signs of the "fever." For five days he continued to work from his home on Church Street; there was some hope that he would recover, as the young priests were now doing. On September 26, however, his condition worsened and he took to his bed.

He was unable to eat, unable to write, and unable to take comfort in the tiny St. Ambrose Chapel, a small room for prayer located just steps from his own bedroom and a place where he had found peaceful retreat during the Famine crisis. He marshalled enough strength to order Hay to send word to Archbishop William Walsh of Halifax to tell Power's mother that her son was gravely ill and near death.[194] At 6:30 on the morning of October 1, 1847, Michael Power died. He had been bishop of Toronto for little more than five years and was only two weeks shy of his 43rd birthday.

Bishop Michael Power

Credit: Archives of the Roman Catholic Archdiocese of Toronto

His death shocked the public. Many in his Church and in the city as a whole pointed to him as a model of individual courage and Christian charity. His legacy thereafter would be that of "a martyr of charity."[195]

The Protestant clergy were not perceived as being as active as their Catholic colleagues at either the hospital or the sheds. Certainly the most active were the Anglicans. About 30 per cent of the arrivals were identified as Protestants, many of them likely members of the Church of Ireland or the Church of England. The Anglicans sponsored a medical dispensary for the poor near the Cathedral and became responsible for burial of all the Protestant dead at their St. James Cemetery.

Bishop John Strachan was active in many of the public meetings held to raise relief funds for the migrants, as were the Reverend Henry J. Grasett, archdeacon of the Cathedral, and the Reverend H.J. Scadding, who himself became ill as a result of making hospital visits. Grasett had a double interest in the hospital. His younger brother, George, was the attending physician until his death on July 16; Henry was a close colleague of Bishop Power, with whom he shared responsibilities on the recently created Board of Education for Canada West.[196]

By August, Henry Grasett had little choice but to make frequent visits to the sheds, given that Scadding had been stricken with the "fever." The *British Colonist* was effusive in its praise of Henry Grasett's self-sacrifice in the wake of his brother's death: "[he] has been most assiduous in his labours among the poor and unfortunate Emigrants, since the establishment of the Hospital, to the great danger to his health …."[197] The Tory newspaper was less kind to Grasett's contemporaries, who it claimed had not been attending to the migrants. Given what they saw as a sorry state of affairs, the paper challenged all Protestant clergy to improve the situation by the time the paper went to press for the next issue. In fairness, many Torontonians would have considered this crisis an "Irish Catholic" problem. Clergy, like most people in the city, feared for their lives.

The work of ordinary Christians, both Protestant and Catholic, was hindered by a fear that either froze them into inaction or prompted them to leave the city hastily. The literate of the city were bombarded each day with newspaper renditions of Board of Health reports of the newly arrived migrants, the sick, the convalescent, the orphaned, and the dead. Health regulations were posted throughout the city: anyone harbouring the sick, carrying the sick or their belongings in their vehicles, or assisting the sick to enter public hostels, rooming houses, or hotels was subject to severe penalties.

The stench of dead bodies fouled the routes of the undertaker's carts, and was particularly noxious to those living and working on King Street East. Added to these constant reminders of death came the fear that a pandemic was about to erupt that would consume the entire city. Although one local newspaper boasted that the city was still ripe for tourists—"our American friends … who will find that Toronto has all the charms she ever had—and more"—most Torontonians were on the edge of panic, unwilling to risk themselves for the "paupers" who arrived daily at Dr. Rees's Wharf. Disgusted, *The Mirror* harangued the locals:

If therefore anyone will escape contagion, let him be clean and
temperate. Shun dirt—but do not run away from your fellow

creature, smitten by the hand of Providence with a disease, which is the product of destitution and privation of every shape. Better to die in the performance of duty, than to preserve life by the cowardly desertion of the afflicted. There are many old wives who dole out the stories of contagion and terror. Tell them to go home and wash their faces and say their prayers.[198]

Donlevy thought that citizens would be safe in the sheds provided that people were clean and temperate to begin with and if they took all due sanitary precautions. What was worrisome to him, however, was that so few within the local population were volunteering to assist the migrants face to face. While wealthy Torontonians gave money to support of the House of Industry, the Refuge for Widows and Orphans, the Emigrant Hospital, and general relief, all of such efforts could easily be done at a distance. People of all income levels kept as far away as they could from the sick and dying.

Donlevy's paper was also very harsh in its assessment of its own Irish Catholic constituency for not having done enough to aid their country-men, particularly when sisters and priests in Montréal and Kingston had laid their lives on the line for those afflicted in the sheds of their cities. Early in the summer, Donlevy appealed to Christian charity to motivate his own community to do more:

People of all income levels kept as far away as they could from the sick and dying.

Are the charities of our Holy Religion dried up? Are our bowls of compassion closed against the cries of our people? Look sir at the squalor and haggard aspect of the poor creatures. Look at their fleshless bodies, and bloodless faces—at their despair, and metal torpor—at their unwashed and unclothed persons, and say we are doing our duty … Sir, there is not an Irish family in this City that could not find some old vestments which would serve these people … The dogs licked the sores of Lazarus at the rich man's gate, and were more merciful than their master. We have less commiseration than the rich man's dogs.[199]

Donlevy, who had identified the fear that gripped the city, hit a nerve with his observations. Roman Catholic citizens who were unwilling to help and who were inclined to flee from their fellow humans in time of need were both counter-witnesses to the Gospel they professed and architects of a social problem greater than they could imagine.

One positive note resonating from the activities of 1847 was the absence of overt discrimination along denominational lines. Although the province had witnessed isolated cases of trouble between Catholics and Protestants earlier in the 1840s, none appeared evident in Toronto at this time. Even when there were some disturbances in a number of towns in New Brunswick during the July 12 Orange parades that celebrated William III's victory at the Boyne, Toronto's parade occurred without incident. According to *The Globe*,

> When the Orangemen paraded through the streets of Toronto …
> with all their frippery and folly, we resolved not to take the
> smallest public notice in their proceedings, but as far as our
> influence extended to let them sink into contempt. Our Roman
> Catholic fellow subjects seem to have acted on this principle,
> and they deserve the highest credit for their forbearance. …
> We believe that the treatment that has been awarded to
> Orangemen this year in the Province, has inflicted a deep
> blow on their unworthy cause.[200]

In a similar spirit of sectarian co-operation, all migrants were accorded equal treatment at hospital facilities under the supervision of the Board of Health. Religious distinctions did not appear in the records of the Convalescent Hospital for its first three weeks of operation; thereafter, the distinction of "Catholic" or "Protestant" was used to assist visiting clergy. Similarly, the Emigrant Hospital began separating Protestant and Catholic patients into sections only to simplify visitations by priests and ministers.[201] In the coming decades, sectarian violence and heated rhetoric between Catholic and Protestant leaders would earn Toronto the nickname "The Belfast of Canada." Thankfully, such a moniker was not warranted during the crisis of 1847.

This time of relative ecumenical spirit and peaceful coexistence between Toronto's Christian leaders provided a timely counterpoint to some citizens' less charitable behaviour during the crisis. Given the manner in which the events of the summer of 1847 unfolded, it was only natural that the local pundits would try to assign blame for the tragedy. It was here, in the finger pointing, that the community became fractured and the old political and nationalistic prejudices reared their ugly heads.

Charles Donlevy's *The Mirror*, the Irish, Catholic reform weekly, was true to form when it took aim at the governments that were promoting the colonization schemes. The paper, which had been founded in 1837, in the period leading up to William Lyon Mackenzie's rebellions against the Tory government, rarely veered away from positions that were embodied in its motto, emblazoned weekly on its masthead: *Dilerant Reges, plectuntur Achivi* (when kings go mad, the subjects wear strait waistcoats).[202] Donlevy lashed out at the captains of the sailing ships for "undernourishment," and at the British navigation legislation that was "no better than the penal laws."[203]

According to *The Mirror*, British Prime Minister Lord John Russell would ultimately have to take responsibility for this disaster, although the editor conceded that the Imperial Government was trying to compensate the colonies for the social and medical assistance that many migrants required upon landing. Nevertheless, when some journalists and civic officials suggested that the entire death toll of the "Black '47" migration—17,365, or "about two out of every eleven souls" who migrated—could have been far worse, Donlevy was indignant. He heaped scorn upon Britain:

> Is this not horrifying? Only think of seventeen thousand human beings sacrificed to the brutal recklessness of a government calling itself Christian! Is such a state of things to be permitted to continue? … We may rest assured that, unless we arouse from our lethargy, next year will be worse than this has been. Canada will be regarded as a good stock farm; a great absorbent of the pauperism of the United Kingdom ….[204]

Donlevy did not stop at criticizing the British government and the Colonial Office. There were plenty of problems evident in the way the Irish migrants were handled when they arrived in Canada.

We admit that the Imperial Government is acting most liberally aiding the sick and destitute emigrants: but let us not forget that with the transportation of the emigrant into our interior, the care of the Imperial Government ceases … We are all loud in our praises of the promptitude of action by our Emigration Agents: but what let us ask, is the state of the case? Go out into the rural districts, and see the dying emigrants perishing by the roadsides, rotting in the woods, or languishing, unsheltered on bare earth, untended and unmourned, and then say what all this comes to. True our large towns have been kept well weeded; but the weeds are only thrown out of our garden into our neighbour's fields, to die or to take roots, as Heaven pleases … Oh! This is a sad system of colonization. It is a sad picture of paternal government ….[205]

In other words, according to Donlevy, the agents and constables working at Rees's Wharf had been very effective at minimizing the effects of pauper immigration to Toronto, in the short term, by simply passing the migrants off to other municipalities. In time, this approach gave rise to a boomerang effect: migrants who had been moved quickly into the countryside and who became ill or failed to find work returned to Toronto in search of medical attention, food, employment, and shelter.

Even the more staid *British Colonist* reported that the Board of Health noted that some migrants who looked well upon arrival eventually returned to the city and found their way to the sheds.[206] Donlevy was not far from the truth when he spoke of the lack of job opportunities for migrants outside Toronto: even Governor General Elgin admitted that Canadian farmers, fearing for their lives, were not hiring the Irish.[207]

One did not have to read an overtly Irish newspaper to sense Canadian anger over the management of immigration in 1847. The weekly *Toronto Examiner* expressed the concerns of many in the city when it observed that the farmers' markets were depressed because "country people" did not wish to venture into the contagion and pall that hung over Toronto. The poorly supplied markets and "flat" business could be blamed only on one thing:

> What is to be the end of this barbarous policy now pursued of pouring in, to the extent from 80,000 to 100,000 of the famished and diseased population of downtrodden Ireland into this province in one season we cannot tell … The landlords of Ireland have sent us their tenantry either to be supported or buried: this is infamous—a simultaneous protest should be transmitted from all parts of Canada and the other Provinces against turning the North American Colonies into a grand Hospital and Poor House for the victims of their oppression. The oppressors of Ireland should be compelled to bear the judgments they have brought upon themselves through their cruelty and injustice—not the inhabitants of these Colonies. Nothing but this will teach them the lessons of humanity and justice.[208]

Increasingly, voices were being heard and opinions being read in Toronto and the rest of Canada West, suggesting that the British government was primarily responsible for remedying an increasingly untenable situation in terms of both the local economy and the health of British subjects in the colonies. *The Globe* agreed, commenting that the "Home Government [had] much to answer for."[209]

Criticisms of the Imperial and local governments by the *Mirror*, *The Globe*, and the *Examiner* were not echoed in Hugh Scobie's *British Colonist*, the local voice of the Tory establishment. Given that its own people—Boulton, Gurnett, Ritchey, and the Grasett brothers—were the principal directors of aid to the migrants, it is not surprising that the *Colonist* was restrained in its critique of the treatment of immigrants. When reading the *Colonist's* report of the minutes of the Toronto Destitute Widow and Orphan Society, one cannot help but detect a more moderate approach to the question of assigning blame:

> Lamentable as is this fact [Canada as a lazaretto], we are not disposed to impute the blame to the Irish landlords, or to any other parties, a want of humanity in shipping off to other lands, more favoured than their own, such of those as lacked the means of subsistence in the "Green Isle": but it is grievous to see so many arrive here, whose advanced age is convincing proof that they have only left the home of their fathers to find a grave in Canada.[210]

The Society directors were prepared, however, to assign blame to the medical authorities in Birkenhead (Liverpool) and other British ports that allowed so many weak and sick migrants to board ships for Canada. Moreover, blame was assigned to ship's captains who provided filthy and poorly ventilated quarters for the migrants in their ships. Even the Canadian government, according to the Society, could have made a better provision of funds, and prepared Canadian ports accordingly for the deluge of humanity that arrived in the spring. Finally, and not atypically, the directors blamed the migrants themselves, whom they described as contributing to the epidemic by their filthy "habits."[211]

Chief Emigrant Agent Anthony Hawke, who shared the politics of *British Colonist* editor Hugh Scobie, cast blame for the 1847 crisis in many directions: the length of time it took migrants to travel from Montréal to the interior; the wretched food on board the ocean vessels; the poor inspection of the potential migrants by physicians in the United Kingdom; and the refusal of some Canadians to employ the immigrants for fear of contracting the dreaded fever. Hawke saved more prolonged complaints, however, for the Irish themselves, some of whom he regarded as lacking in industry, honesty, and ambition.[212] Many of the Irish migrants, he claimed, were "diseased in body, belonging generally to the lowest class of unskilled laborers—very few of them are fit for farm servants ...."[213] Hawke was even critical of those Irish who were able to subsist in their new land:

> Added to this they are generally dirty in their habits and unreasonable in their expectations as to wages. They appear to

possess but little ambition or desire to adapt themselves to the new state of things with which they are surrounded. The few who possess any money invariably secret it and will submit to any amount of suffering or have recourse to begging in the streets and the most humiliating and pertinacious supplications to obtain a loaf of bread from the Board of Health or Emigrant agents rather than part with a shilling. Hitherto such people have been the exceptions to the general character of immigration, but this year they constitute a large majority.[214]

"… [the Irish] are generally dirty in their habits and unreasonable in their expectations as to wages."

Such negative images of the Irish were not uncommon in the United Kingdom even prior to the Famine, nor unknown in British North America. But the manner in which the Famine migration to Canada appeared to confirm previous stereotypes and suspicions would go far beyond the privately articulated frustrations of the Chief Emigrant Agent.

This temptation to blame the Famine migrants themselves for their condition would be repeated in a public meeting held in Toronto in September 1847 to address the mounting immigrant crisis. On Saturday, September 18, Mayor William Boulton convened a public gathering. The cream of Toronto's civic and religious leadership was present. In addition to the mayor, attendees included Chief Justice John Beverly Robinson, Board of Health Chair, George Gurnett, Anglican Bishop John Strachan, local philanthropist and Catholic convert John Elmsley, and Roman Catholic Bishop Michael Power. Participants at the meeting appeared to reach consensus on a great variety of issues: securing better shelter for the migrants, encouraging the employment of the Irish as soon as possible, and lobbying the Canadian government for additional funds to sustain municipal relief projects.

During the meeting there may have been a discussion of how the migrants themselves were at fault for the epidemic that was raging in the hospital and sheds, for at one point Michael Power rose to his feet and addressed the assembly. He spoke of witnessing the sick and weak boarding the ships when he was in Dublin that spring, adding that even those who were in good health in Dublin appeared ill upon arrival in

Liverpool. This "fever" was deceptive: one day a person appeared healthy and was seen as such by medical officers; days later, this same person was ill.

Power said that the same problem was evident at Grosse Île, where the healthy were cleared of quarantine, only to fall ill by the time they reached Montréal or points farther inland. Power made it clear to all present: "the disease seemed to be of that insidious character, as to baffle all the skill that might be employed in treating for its cure and it did not seem to be affected by change of season."[215] The Irish themselves were not to be blamed for this disease; they were victims. The irony of Power's eloquence at this meeting was lost neither to contemporary observers nor to historians. Within two weeks, on October 1, he himself was dead from typhus.

Soon after, on October 29, Edward McElderry, the tireless emigration sub-agent, also died of "fever." He left behind his pregnant wife, Roseanna, and their seven young children, the eldest of whom was only thirteen. To his credit, A.B. Hawke immediately requested a lump sum allowance for the grieving widow and her family, whom he described as "entirely destitute." Claiming that McElderry had been underpaid, given the circumstances of the Toronto wharves, his 10 shilling per day salary should be raised to 15, retroactive to May 1, 1847. The difference between the original salary and the adjusted one (£46) should be paid out to Roseanna.

In a strongly worded letter to the Governor General, Hawke expressed great admiration for a man he once characterized as "a stranger" and "unscholarly": "he was a good man in every relation of life and has certainly fallen a victim of duty. Had he less zeal he would have given himself time to recover from the effects of fever, but he persisted in working beyond his strength and the dysentery set in fatally."[216]

Hawke's request was denied. Stephen De Vere, the outspoken critic of the conditions on the ships from Ireland to British North America, intervened, but to no avail. When McElderry's widow petitioned the Governor General directly for a pension, given the circumstances of her husband's untimely death while in the employ of the Crown, she was refused. R.B. Sullivan, a secretary to the Governor General, wrote to George Gurnett that many public servants had died in the dispatch of their duties, so that Mrs. McElderry was not entitled to funds that other grieving families were not receiving. McElderry's widow, however, was at least able to secure her own guardianship of her children.[217]

By the autumn of 1847, the Board of Health and civic officials were concerned about how the large numbers of inmates at the sheds and hospitals would be accommodated during the coming winter. The resolutions that emerged from the public meeting on September 20 had been transmitted by Mayor Boulton to the Provincial Secretary, Dominick Daly, but the government gave no official response until October 11. Citizens of Toronto would find Daly's point-by-point assessment of the resolutions wanting.

The charges that sick immigrants were being allowed to slip through medical authorities downstream from Toronto would have to be formally investigated. The barracks facilities would soon be reassumed by new troops assigned to Toronto, so that the plan of expanding convalescent and refuge facilities was blocked. Moreover, requests for provincial funds to erect an asylum or "North House" to the hospital were being directed to the office of Chief Emigrant Agent, A.B. Hawke.[218]

This was not the first time the Toronto Board of Health had been frustrated by the central government. In August, A.C. Buchanan had been so displeased with Toronto's spending habits that he sent Hawke on a mission to audit the Board of Health ledgers. Of particular concern was the issue of the purchase of 258 gallons of wine and twelve gallons of brandy for the treatment of 500 patients. Apparently, Montréal's Board of Health had needed only 10 gallons of brandy to treat nearly 1,300 patients.[219] Toronto's Board was exonerated when it threatened to resign en masse if Hawke continued interfering in the purchasing prerogatives of Board or tried to micromanage the "higher" wages offered to physicians in the Toronto facilities.[220]

Buchanan and Hawke were not simply being fiscally parsimonious. The press had already alerted the public to certain anomalies in the operations of the Board and its associates. While the pandemic had brought out the best in some of its citizens, not all activities undertaken by the Board were beyond reproach. Local politicians and civic officials appeared enmeshed in the tight webs of patronage and cronyism endemic in colonial politics, and were not above securing their own profits in the midst of the crisis. A relative of the mayor, Henry John Boulton, was able to rent out some of his own properties on King Street in order to expand the Emigrant Hospital.

John Ritchey, a former city alderman, landowner, contractor, and colleague of Boulton and Gurnett, was able to secure all of the contracts for the building of the hospital sheds; Ritchey also got the contracts for building the Provincial Lunatic Asylum, where several of the Famine migrants found rest.[221] The old connections of the Family Compact were still very much alive ten years after William Lyon Mackenzie's failed rebellions.

Moreover, there emerged the controversy over the miscount of patients at the hospital, the *Mirror's* and Dr. Rankin's questioning of the alcohol consumption by migrants or others, and the tale of Ryan's hearse, where one coffin held two corpses. While Gurnett, Boulton, and others might have resented Hawke's sticking his nose into things, various shady happenstances warranted some degree of external scrutiny of the Toronto operation.

As the shipping season wound down and numbers of arriving migrants dwindled in some locations, Hawke began to close Boards of Health in an effort to save money. Although he pledged that no Board would be closed if it meant "any additional suffering to immigrants or injury to the public," by late September, many of the 28 Boards of Health in smaller towns such as Chatham, Amherstburg, and Guelph were dissolved and their patients sent to the nearest existing Board of Health.[222] Closures at Peterborough, Port Hope, Cobourg, Newmarket, and Barrie meant additional strain in Toronto.

Given the huge costs incurred by the provincial government, the refusal of Mrs. McElderry's request for financial support for her family appeared in keeping with needed fiscal restraint. Governor General Elgin and his Privy Council well knew that the expenditures of local

Boards of Health had far exceeded the original budgets. By December, eighteen of the 28 Boards of Health reported expenses of £32,762 for the season, while the local emigration agencies in Toronto, Hamilton, Cobourg, Kingston, and Bytown had spent £14,832 for food and transportation.

In Toronto alone, McElderry and his successor, Roache Hayes, had incurred transportation and food costs for indigent migrants of over £2,481, or nearly seventeen per cent of the entire Emigrant Agency's expenses for these items.[223] The Elgin administration looked to the Colonial Office for redress of these debts; in 1848, the Imperial Government compensated the Canadian government for immigrant expenses to the tune of £150,000,[224] but thereafter, the Province of Canada was virtually on its own.

Approximately 1,124 of the 38,560 migrants had died and were buried in Toronto.

Elgin was of a mind that Canada would shape emigration policy with a greater degree of autonomy from that point on, but revenues and expenses for emigration would have to be determined in Canada and come out of the Canadian government's budget.[225] The proposal to raise the per capita tax on migrants and the penalties on ship captains in violation of the Passenger Act appeared to have influenced migration trends.[226] Given this legislation, Earl Grey, at the Colonial Office, indicated that Britain would no more pay emigrant expenses to Québec than it would to New York.[227]

It was fortunate for the public purse that under these new circumstances, trans-Atlantic migration to British North America trailed off in the coming shipping seasons. In 1848, British and Irish migration to British North America amounted to only 31,065, of whom about half (16,535) sailed from Irish ports;[228] in 1849, the number of migrants would increase to about 41,367, but never again would it come close to the overwhelming numbers of "Black '47."[229]

When the final reports on the tragedy of 1847 in Toronto were issued in early 1848, the staggering toll of the "year of the Irish" was graphically revealed. Approximately 1,124 of the 38,560 migrants had died and were buried in Toronto.[230] Three in every four migrants were Roman Catholic, a striking change to the nature of Irish migration to

Upper Canada, which up until that year had been primarily Protestant. In February, the *British Colonist* reported that 757 Irish were buried in the Catholic cemetery, 305 were buried at St. James Anglican Cemetery, and 50 persons were buried in the Potter's Field of York County.

With the sickness and death of 1847 behind them, local politicians began to prepare for the coming season, petitioning that the British no longer consider the province of Upper Canada as Ireland's graveyard. Their fears that the dire events of 1847 would be repeated did not materialize the following year; migrants from Ireland in 1848 preferred to travel to the tidewater ports in the United States. The fact still remained, however, that at the end of 1847, one fifth of those migrants who left Famine conditions in Ireland for safe haven in British North America were dead. That the fever epidemic also carried off doctors, clergy, orderlies, and nurses who had tended to the sick and dying only deepened the extent of the tragedy.

CHAPTER FIVE

Memory and Commemoration

WHILE THE END of the shipping season in November brought a halt to the reception of new migrants, the city of Toronto still faced considerable challenges to its medical infrastructure and its self-image as a growing, progressive North American city. As the census takers made clear in 1851–52, the social and religious demographics of the city had been altered by the influx of migrants in 1847 and the boomerang effect of migrants returning to the city the following year, after their unsuccessful sojourn in the countryside. The city's population was now more visibly Catholic, Irish, and, for want of a better word, destitute. Hundreds of sick and convalescing immigrants lingered in the "fever hospital," while dozens more local citizens who had come down with typhus occupied expanded facilities of the Toronto General Hospital.

Reactions to their harrowing experience varied. For a few priests and bishops, the Famine migration inspired a sense of providential mission: the Irish would work to convert the Protestant continent to the "true faith."[231] For some Irish Catholics, the Famine migration would become a touchstone of identity, providing a strong bond from a collective sense of suffering, out of which, it was hoped, some good might come.

Some of them would come to view the Famine as the most sordid chapter yet in Britain's longstanding oppression of the Irish people. Remembering the Famine was to remember the real enemies of Ireland. Such was the case of Patrick Boyle, editor of Toronto's *Irish Canadian*. In 1866, he attacked what he saw as the real cause of the Famine tragedy in a nationalist tone that was reminiscent of Young Ireland's John Mitchel:

> Where are the friends of our youth, the classmates of our schoolboy days? Alas! Some are laid beneath the green turf of their native soil, or slept at the bottom of the Atlantic wave, the victims of an unnatural and unchristian system of government, which dried up their vitals by the horrid process of starvation, or drove them in search of new habitation, ... amid the perils of the deep. Others wander the four corners of the globe, seeking recognition for their talents and labour denied them by the paternal government of England, and making for themselves a home and competence by ancient toil and preserving unwearied industry. To this latter class the Irish of America belong ... Assemble then fellow countrymen, and testify to your unalterable love of the land that bore you, and show by your presence that it is still your pride and proud privilege to participate in the glories of St. Patrick's Day.[232]

Such incendiary rhetoric did nothing to stem the suspicion and hostility brewing against the Irish within other sectors of Toronto. For some Protestant citizens, the Famine and its aftermath provided a host of negative images of their new neighbours—images that would persist for generations, becoming hardened stereotypes of the Irish Catholic men and women in the province.[233]

Many surviving migrants bore psychological scars. The stresses of leaving one's home, compounded by the tribulations resulting from a desperate voyage across the north Atlantic, only to be faced with debilitating illness and the loss of loved ones would put a strain on even the strongest person. The case of little Catherine Burns is but one example.

In June 1847, as the family travelled from Lachine to Cornwall, two-year-old Catherine developed a "bowel complaint" and died. The distraught parents, unable to bury the child immediately, placed her in a box, intending to inter her remains at Kingston. When told by authorities there that if he left the ship he would be shot, Catherine's father was forced to take her corpse to Toronto. Lacking the money to pay for her burial, Burns proceeded to Hamilton. En route, he tossed the box overboard. Burns was charged and reprimanded, but later freed. In the meantime, his wife died.[234]

Equally gripping stories began to trickle into Toronto papers from nearby areas. In Lloydtown, north of Toronto, an Irish emigrant slit his own throat in February 1848 with a razor, severing his windpipe. He had lost his wife and children to "emigrant fever" during the summer of 1847 and had been "in a desponding state" ever since.[235]

Another man, Thomas Brennan, lived through the Famine, lost his 10-acre farm on the Mahon Estate, and survived the trans-Atlantic journey on the *Virginius*, recognized as one of the most notorious vessels to cross the Atlantic in 1847. At journey's end, seventeen Brennans from Roscommon were among the 267 steerage passengers who died at sea or in quarantine. Thomas Brennan's wife survived the voyage, but died at Grosse Île. He and his children moved on to Queenston, on the Niagara Peninsula. In 1848, he was tried and hanged for the murder of his friend Patrick O'Connor, Patrick's wife, Mary, and their young son.[236]

Other traumatized Irish arrived at the doors of the Toronto Asylum. From August 25, 1847, to January 10, 1848, ten Irish migrants were admitted to the mental hospital. Some were transferred from Kingston; all were paupers. Eight of the ten were under 30 years of age, and one, Hanna Heron, suffered from amnesia.[237]

The question of the dozens of widows and orphans left in Toronto was often overlooked in the process of settling the surviving migrants. The Widows and Orphans Asylum on Bathurst Street processed 627 persons made destitute by the deaths of parents or spouses. Only four of those admitted to the Asylum were of non-Irish origin. Until the institution closed at the end of May 1848, Asylum officials arranged

The question of the dozens of widows and orphans left in Toronto was often overlooked in the process of settling the surviving migrants.

for children and young women to be sent to relatives or to families needing domestic servants, farm labourers, or assistance around homes or businesses.[238]

In one instance, Robert Keenan of Adjala Township, an area with a high concentration of Irish Catholic settlers from earlier migrations, asked Father Thaddeus Kirwin of St. Paul's Parish for nineteen Catholic orphans to be sent to Catholic farm families in Adjala and Tecumseth townships. Keenan's request, which was mostly for boys ages four to eight, was accompanied by the assurance that "the above named men [who had asked for the orphans] are of good moral character and industrious habits and in comfortable circumstances."[239]

Keenan's request was merely the tip of a much larger adoption process; from September 1847 to May 1848, the civil authorities changed the lives of 197 children ages four and up and young widows up to age 35 by arranging their adoption, indentured service, or residence with families in Toronto and hinterland.[240] Father Amable Charest and Father Thaddeus Kirwin were entrusted to deliver many of the children to their new homes, which suggests that the Church saw fit to make certain that Catholic children (the majority of the orphans) and Catholic widows would be placed in Catholic homes, farms, and businesses.

With each child, the Widows and Orphans Association specified the length of the contract, the rate of pay (where applicable), and the amount of bedding and suits of clothing the families and employers were to give to their wards. Many of the contracts involving adolescents were to be terminated when the individual turned 21, at which point a specified remittance, sometimes $100, was to be awarded to the young person to conclude the contract. While the story of the integration of the Grosse Île orphans into French Canadian society is fairly well known,[241] there is little record of what happened to women and children who were stranded in Toronto after the death of parents, spouses, and siblings in 1847.

The psychological impact on Irish Famine migrants to Toronto was clearly substantial, which may explain why many of them did not seem to linger in the city. Yet the demographic change to the city is, at first glance, deceiving. By 1848, 35,650 of the migrants (26,700 by boat to Hamilton and Niagara; 8,950 by land) had moved beyond Toronto in search of relatives or work elsewhere in British North America or the United States. Aside from the 1,005 immigrants still housed in the Emigrant Hospital, fever sheds, Convalescent Hospital, and Orphan's Asylum, both *The Globe* and *The Mirror* reported that only 781 migrants from "Black '47" had taken up lodgings in the city. Things seemed to be getting back to normal.

The demand made on health-care facilities designed for a population of around 20,000 was staggering, yet impressive. During the sailing season of 1847, the Emigrant Hospital had admitted 4,355 patients, of whom 863 had died of their afflictions; 2,869 persons had been discharged. The legacy of ill health among the emigrants, however, carried over well into 1848; by February, 413 patients remained in the Emigrant Hospital and 210 in the convalescent hospital.[242]

Meanwhile, to the consternation of municipal officials, some of the emigrants who had been dispatched to the country started to filter back into the city. By February 1848, fears of a relapse of the typhus epidemic appeared justified as 1,074 Irish migrants returned to the sheds. Two in every three became dependent on public charity.[243] Dozens of other migrants returned to Toronto when job prospects in the countryside failed to materialize. For many labourers, the major city in the region likely seemed the only possibility for gainful employment now that the fall harvests were already in the barns.

While the Famine migration did not change the settlement grid of Canada West appreciably, it certainly altered the religious balance in Toronto for the next decade. In 1841, the Roman Catholic population of Toronto stood at 2,401—little more than 14 per cent of Toronto's total population of 14,249.[244] By 1848, the year immediately after the Famine migration, Catholics accounted for 5,903 persons, or 25.1 per cent of the city's population of 23,503.[245] This percentage increased slightly several years later, when the Census of 1851–52 reported that Catholics now formed 25.8 per cent (or 7,940) of the city's population of 30,775.

Perhaps more startling was the fact that the number of Irish-born persons recorded in the city between 1848 and 1851, had skyrocketed by a whopping 600 per cent, from 1,695 to 11,305.[246] Both physically and psychologically, the Irish had now become a significant presence in Toronto; in terms of numbers, they were now one of the largest ethno-religious groups in the city.

One institution affected by the boomerang effect and therefore by the large numbers of paupers who remained in the city was the House of Industry. The British-style workhouse provided food and shelter in exchange for labour; many Irish, both Catholic and Protestant, availed themselves of these facilities in "Black '47" and beyond. Between June and December 1847, 202 persons were admitted to the House of Industry; of this number, 152 (75 per cent) were Irish. Over half of these Irish (54.6 per cent) were Anglicans, which cast doubt on the notion that Irishness, poverty, and Catholicism were synonymous.[247]

In January 1848, 142 Irish, constituting approximately 80 per cent of all the admissions, were recorded in the ledger of the House of Industry. The numerous orphans and single women were quickly moved to the Widows and Orphans Asylum; single men and families (including single-parent families) remained. The most remarkable entry during the winter was the admission of Irish Catholic widow Anne Maguire, who brought her nine children into the refuge with her. No other family admitted during the rest of the year rivalled hers in size.[248] Having come through so many trials in the journey from Ireland to Canada, all Maguire could do to save her family was to throw them on the charity of the citizens of Toronto.

Unfortunately, the circumstances of "Black '47" appeared to reinforce hardened stereotypes of the Irish Catholics as lazy, ignorant, bellicose, and intemperate paupers.[249] This prominent negative image of the Irish could not have come at a worse time for sectarian relations in the Province of Canada. By 1850, the Protestant world had become deeply troubled by the resurgence of Roman Catholicism in Europe under its young, dynamic and charismatic leader, Pope Pius IX. When he was elected pontiff in 1846, having succeeded the noted conservative and ultramontane Gregory XVI, some observers had viewed Giovanni Mastai-Ferretti as a "liberal" or *politicante*. Early in his pontificate, his reforms to the physical infrastructure of the Papal States, social legislation, and the updating of his parliament appeared to be signs that the early indications about "Pio Nono" were correct.

But as a result of the European revolutions of 1848 and the temporary occupation of Rome by Garibaldi's nationalist and liberal forces, Pius IX's tenure took a much more conservative tack. Having reclaimed Rome with the assistance of French troops, Pius and his ultramontane entourage set about asserting the Catholic presence in the mission fields and in countries in Europe that had been strong preserves of Protestantism. In 1855, he re-established the Catholic Church in Calvinist Holland.

The most threatening action had come five years before, when Pius appointed Nicholas Wiseman, the Archbishop of Westminster, to a newly instituted Catholic hierarchy in England, the heart of the British Empire. Protestant fears were not relieved when Wiseman, contrary to what his surname might suggest, issued a notice to Protestantism in his *From Outside the Flaminian Gate* that suggested that Catholicism was on the move in Britain. Such "Papal Aggression" came at a time when the High Churchmen and the Tractarians, centred at Oxford University, appeared to be undermining Anglicanism with their insistence on returning to more "Catholic" traditions within the Church of England. To the literate Protestant in Upper Canada, the open Bible and Reformation principles would soon be under attack in Canada.[250]

Both physically and psychologically, the Irish had now become a significant presence in Toronto ....

These fears of "papal aggression" abroad were made more threatening by the seeming "Rome Rule" that reared its head in the Parliament of Canada in the 1850s. In 1841, the Union of the Canadas had at its heart a rather dysfunctional constitution that grafted the provinces of Lower and Upper Canada together in a single legislature. Each former colony would be given equal representation in the new assembly, but for all intents and purposes, each ministry was a joint effort, with each "section" having its own ministers to manage the affairs of state.

Although the sections were officially called Canada West and Canada East, in the vernacular they were still popularly referred to as Upper Canada and Lower Canada, respectively. By the 1850s, no government could form with any confidence for a long duration unless there was a solid block of French Canadian Catholic support from among the members from Canada East. For Protestants, this arrangement was highly problematic when the issue of publicly funded Catholic schools for Canada West came to debate in the house. In 1855, French Canadian Conservatives voted solidly for such schools and their extended denominational rights, even though a majority of the members from Canada West, most of whom were Protestant, voted against sectarian establishments. The mere fact that a French Canadian Catholic majority from one section, with the assistance of a minority of members from the other section, could force Catholic schools on Protestant Upper Canada was tantamount to "papal aggression" in Canada.[251]

The presence of such a visible group of Irish Catholics in Canada West's largest and fastest-growing city did not allay Protestant fears about a Catholic agenda. With events in Europe and Canada both suggesting that Catholics were a menace, it comes as no surprise that the Famine Irish could become targets for the religious bigot and the small-minded politician. Added to the mix was the new bishop of Toronto, replacing Michael Power, in 1850. Bishop Armand de Charbonnel was a French nobleman who became publicly assertive about Catholic schools and Catholic rights in his diocese. Toronto found itself a hotbed of sectarian tension; the image of the Irish was not far from the epicentre of the trouble.

One of the most striking residual effects of "Black '47" was the hostile way the local population viewed all Irish thereafter: as a problem and an impediment to progress rather than as a blessing to their community. Political cartoons lampooned the Irish by means of the "Paddy" stereotype: ragged, simian looking, feckless, and poor. J.W. Bengough, one of the country's leading illustrators, often used the "Paddy" as his symbol of hard times. A decade later, Conservative Party pundits alleged that the Liberal *Globe* was hostile to Catholics and the Irish, as evidenced by comments like this one:

> Irish beggars are to be met everywhere, and they are as ignorant
> and vicious as they are poor. They are lazy, improvident, and

unthankful; they fill our poorhouses and our prisons, and are as brutish in their superstition as Hindoos."[252]

The Famine moment left similarly powerful impressions upon the local Catholic population. Pre-Famine Irish Catholic migrants would come to identify the suffering of their brothers and sisters as common suffering. In time, the Famine experience would come to be the touch-stone for Irish identity in central Canada. Given the horrors that had transpired in the homeland and the trials of the new world, it is little wonder that the Irish in Canada came to see themselves as a people more sinned against than sinning.

It would be at least two generations before the descendants of the Irish Catholics—both pre-Famine and Famine migrants—would integrate effectively into the social, political, and economic life of Toronto. By 1920, Irish descendants could be found in all of Toronto's neighbourhoods, from the "tenements of the Ward" to the forested lanes and manorial homes of Rosedale. By that time, a majority of the descendants owned their own homes and could be found among all the vocations and occupations evident in a growing industrial city: labourers, craftsmen, clerks, telephone operators, brewers, bankers, physicians, and politicians. Increasingly, Catholics intermarried with Protestants and died with them in proportionate numbers on the fields of France and Flanders.[253]

The Famine memory began to fade in some areas of the country as each generation gave way to the next and as Canadians of Irish descent intermarried with persons from other cultural groups. Such was not the case in some parts of Québec, particularly in Montréal and Quebec City, where Irish Catholic descendents found themselves in a double minority situation[254]—a linguistic minority in a Church dominated by French Canadians, and a religious minority in anglophone communities dominated by Protestants. In these urban Québec landscapes, "Irishness" easily emerged as the default identity and the Ancient Order of Hibernians (AOH), one of its most prominent agencies.[255]

In 1897, inspired by Jeremiah Gallagher, the Quebec City AOH, which was appalled at the state of the burial grounds on Grosse Île at the 50th anniversary ceremonies for "Black '47," launched an ambitious commemoration project. When it was unveiled on August 15, 1909, the mammoth Celtic cross on Telegraph Hill, Grosse Île, became Canada's best-known Famine commemoration site. Like many memorials to the Irish Famine erected in the early 20th century, the inscription (written in Irish) exposes the emergent nationalism of some of the memorial's benefactors and supporters. The Irish dedication, which is different from accompanying inscriptions in French and English, is pointed and political:

> Thousands of the children of the Gael were lost on this island while fleeing from foreign tyrannical laws and an artificial famine in the years 1847–48. God bless them. This stone was erected to their memory and in honour of them by the Gaels of America. God save Ireland![256]

By this inscription, the AOH mirrored the manner in which nationalists in Ireland had woven the Famine into the more general narrative of self-determination and home rule from Britain.

In the1990s, the Canadian government's attempts to reconstruct the quarantine station at Grosse Île and designate it a national park, and the coincidental memorial celebrations of the 150th anniversary of the potato blight in Ireland once again brought to the fore the issue of the Famine. Many Canadians of Irish descent, particularly first-generation Irish Canadians, feared that the island would be turned into a theme park. They argued loudly at public meetings in 1992 and 1993 that Grosse Île be respected as a national monument to the Irish migration.[257] Once again, the Famine moment tended to overshadow the historical realities that Irish migration had taken place over centuries, not just in 1847.

The public discussion had a number of positive effects, however. In 1994, Irish President Mary Robinson visited the site to pay tribute to those who lost their lives in the Famine.[258] A Toronto organization called Action Grosse Île raised awareness through public lectures and an essay contest for secondary school students. In 1997, Parks Canada unveiled the Grosse Île Quarantine Station and Irish Memorial. The site allows visitors to view the reconstructed lazarettos (fever sheds) and pay their respects at the burial sites of more than 5,000 victims of "Black '47" who perished while quarantined on the island. This memorial in the middle of the St. Lawrence River has inspired the construction of other memorials across Canada.

Famine commemorations have been erected across eastern Canada in the key ports of call where the Irish first set foot in Canada during the Famine years. Toronto's first Famine memorial was erected in 1932 in front of St. Paul's Church on Power Street. The memorial commemorates Bishop Michael Power, who died serving the migrants in 1847, and the Catholic Famine victims buried nearby in unmarked graves.

In 1998, some of these unmarked graves were unearthed when work was being done on pipes outside St. Paul's School; once the site was restored and the tarmac replaced, Action Grosse Île, in its continuing efforts to raise awareness of the Irish Famine and contemporary famines elsewhere in the world, installed a small plaque to honour the dead of "Black '47." (For more information on the graves, see Appendix D.)

More recently, plaques commemorating the Famine have been erected at the corner of King and John Streets, across from the site of the Emigration Hospital. The Black Rock memorial in Montréal commemorates the thousands who died in the fever sheds at Point St. Charles, and whose graves now lie beneath industrial and railway lands. More recent Celtic crosses have been erected in Halifax and Kingston; their inscriptions do not contain nationalist indignation. In Miramichi, New Brunswick, an Irish historical park was built on Middle Island to commemorate the island's use as a quarantine station in 1847.

The most recent commemoration of the Famine appeared in 2007, at Toronto Harbour. The memorial was conceived by Robert Kearns, a local Irish-born entrepreneur and philanthropist who was moved and inspired by the seven bronze images marking the departure in 1847 of Famine migrants and installed at Dublin's Custom House Quay. Irish sculptor Rowan Gillespie had cast seven figures of Irish refugees headed

Famine commemorations have been erected across eastern Canada in the key ports of call where the Irish first set foot in Canada during the Famine years.

to the Americas as the city's official memorialization project to mark the 150th anniversary of the beginning of the Famine in 1845.

Kearns and his brother Jonathan, a respected Toronto architect, gathered a team of like-minded Irish expatriates and Irish Canadians to create a memorial to the Famine at Toronto Harbour. The Ireland Park Famine Memorial was officially opened by Irish President Mary McAleese, Ontario Premier Dalton McGuinty, Canadian Federal Finance Minister Jim Flaherty, and Toronto Mayor David Miller on June 21, 2007.

The Park contains new work by Gillespie—this time, images of five of the migrants arriving—in addition to a massive Kilkenny limestone wall, upon which the names of over 660 Famine victims are inscribed, and a column with interactive computer screens that offer background information on the Irish and Toronto stories.

Unlike other memorials, however, the Park allows the names of the dead to speak for themselves. There is no overt political message to the site. The Foundation states openly in its promotional literature that in addition to dedicating itself to preserving the memory of the victims of the Irish Famine, it aims to "Celebrate the contribution of the Irish who went on to make meaningful contributions to Toronto and Canada" and remains committed to "Re-enforce the Canadian traditions of welcoming waves of immigrants from around the world."[259]

While implicitly suggesting the success of subsequent generations of the Irish in Canada, the Toronto memorial in no way emphasizes the rags-to-riches motif found in recent memorial sculptures in Boston (1998), Philadelphia (2003), and Providence (2008). In the American memorials, the Famine is a backdrop against which the rise of Irish Catholics and their integration into the mainstream of American life, in all of its dimensions, can be set.[260]

The Ireland Park memorial also stands in contrast to earlier Irish memorials at places such as Ballyseedy, outside of Tralee, County Kerry, where the Famine and Irish revolutionary narratives are intertwined in the 1950s work of Breton sculptor Yann Goulet. Prominent at the centre of that monument are four figures: a dying, emaciated man tended to by a woman showing a baby, symbolic of the new Ireland, and a young man in 20th-century garb marching with determination into the future. The dying Famine victim appears to give reason and purpose for the young man's determination to win Ireland's freedom from foreign tyranny—a message, no doubt, from the nationalistic Goulet that there were compelling and long-standing historical reasons for the Irish to overthrow British rule.

Moreover, the memorial is on the site of the Ballyseedy massacre, which claimed the lives of Republican soldiers at the hands of Free State troops during the Irish Civil War, 1922–1923. Here, in stone and metal, the Famine memory is woven into a larger narrative that speaks to the centuries-old occupation of Ireland by Britain, the dire consequences of which—starvation in the 1840s—were part of a battery of justifications to take up arms in 1916 and win Ireland's autonomy by 1923.

Credit: M. McGowan

Memorial at Ballyseedy, Kerry

This type of nationalist narrative, however, did not translate into the memorials unveiled in Ireland for the 150th anniversary of the Famine, or *Gorta Mor*. John Behan's "Famine Ship" was unveiled by President Mary Robinson in County Mayo on July 20, 1997. This poignant and macabre bronze sculpture of a ship features skeletons flying about the rigging. The fact the National Famine Memorial sits looking out to sea, close to the foot of Croagh Patrick, the most sacred and ancient of Irish Christian pilgrimage sites, speaks volumes.

The Famine memory touches the heart of a contemporary sense of Irish history and collective self-understanding. Erected amid the roar of the Celtic Tiger and its accompanying economic prosperity, the monument's inscription moves towards a new understanding of lessons learned from the Famine. Yes, it is dedicated to those who died, suffered, and emigrated during the Irish Famine of 1847, but it also is dedicated to famine victims everywhere. This latter perspective marks the new way to memorialize the Famine: remember the past so it does not happen again.

National Famine Monument, County Mayo

Credit: E.J.P. McGowan

Credit: M. McGowan

Famine Walk Memorial, Doolough Valley, County Mayo

Not far away, in the Doolough Valley, where 600 starving tenants marched about 10 miles (15 km) from Louisburgh to Delphi in March 1849 to beg for food from the landlord, a similar message is found on a simpler memorial. A small, rough-hewn stone Celtic cross is dedicated to the "pilgrims" who, having been refused sustenance by the landlord, died by the hundreds in a snowstorm while trying to return home. The inscription, which includes a closing quotation from Mahatma Gandhi, reads,

> To Commemorate the Hungry Poor Who Walked Here in 1849 and Walk the Third World Today. Freedom for South Africa, 1994. How Can Men Feel Themselves Honoured by the Humiliation of Their Fellow Beings.

In his groundbreaking essay on Famine commemoration, Peter Gray identifies the shift in commemoration that took place as a result of the commitment of the state and two non-governmental organizations

(NGOs) to international development: Concern, and Action from Ireland (AFrI). Gray comments,

> It would be churlish to criticize the work of the NGOs in raising consciousness about global injustice and poverty. At a political level, one can only applaud their success in externalising and giving an active meaning to Famine commemoration, particularly in the context of a society that is itself now firmly in the leading group of first world economies.[261]

The connection between Irish Famine history and the present was not lost on Irish President Mary Robinson during the preparations leading up to the sesquicentennial celebrations. Robinson offered considerable impetus in broadening the scope of Irish Famine commemoration to include modern geopolitical realities.[262]

This sense of purpose in alleviating the pain and misery of famine today has also become evident in the interpretations offered by curator Luke Dodd at the National Famine Museum at Strokestown Park, County Roscommon. Here the lives of tenants and their landlords, the Mahons, are recounted in great detail without resorting to a thesis of victimization. The museum takes great pains to identify and examine living conditions, the labouring poor, international development projects, and the ongoing struggle to survive among the people in Eritrea, Mali, Sudan, Ethiopia, and parts of South Asia.[263]

One must avoid making uncritical, ahistorical, and simplistically sentimental analogies between the causes and character of the Irish Famine and the present calamities. At the same time, one need not ignore the fact that human self-interest, callousness, political ideology, and an uncritical belief in laissez-faire economic policies continue to threaten the lives of innocent people. Perhaps the old adage that those who fail to learn their history doom themselves to repeat it deserves some sober second thought.

In Canada, the Famine is part of a much larger canvas of Irish migration and settlement in Canada. As horrific and dramatic as the events of 1847 were, the Irish story in Toronto and Canada is much larger and more complex than the events in any given calendar year. Irish migrants had mingled among the soldiers and settlers of New France and were active in the Newfoundland fishery long before the Famine. Irish migrants, Catholic and Protestant, spent much of the first half of the nineteenth century carving out the farmsteads and establishing the settlement grid of parts of New Brunswick, rural Québec, and Upper Canada, and were among those who provided remittance payments[264] to those eager to escape the Famine in 1847.

Many migrants of the Famine period chose British North America because it contained well-established Irish communities, many of which had become home to relatives and friends. Irish men and women who made their mark on Canadian society, industry, religious life, and public service came from a rich and varied background. Some crossed the Atlantic in the Famine period; many others left Ireland under more positive circumstances.

And yet there is no denying that the lens of 1847 has been a powerful one. It reminds us of the hardness that often burdens the human heart, the fragility of human existence, and the courage of those who saw fit to serve their neighbours, even at the cost of their own lives.

Appendix A

Emigration and Deaths,
United Kingdom to British North America, 1847

Particular	Canada	New Brunswick	Total
Embarked	89,738	17,074	106,812
Died on Passage	5,293	823	6,116
Died in Quarantine	3,452	697	4,149
Died in Hospital	6,585	595	7,180
Total Deaths	**15,330**	**2,115**	**17,445**

Notes: A.C. Buchanan, the Chief Emigrant Agent in Québec, claimed that 6/7 or 85.7 per cent of migrants arriving at that port were Irish. An additional 2,000 arrived at Halifax, 993 at Newfoundland, and 536 in Prince Edward Island, making the grand total for British North America 110,341. There is some question about the children, who were counted differently by officials at ports of departure. Children under twelve months, for instance, were not counted, and children under fourteen years were sometimes counted as a half "statute adult."

Sources: Library and Archives Canada (LAC), Colonial Office, 384/82, Colonial Land and Emigration Commission, Eighth General Report (June 1848), 15–17. Reel 1746, frames 166–8. *Mirror*, 20 August 1847.

Appendix B

Arrivals at the Toronto Convalescent Hospital,
6 August 1847 to 26 May 1848

Month	Total Admitted	Adults	Children	Orphans	Widows	Protestant	Catholic	In Hospital at Month's End
August 1847	462	273	189	39	8	14	62*	302
September	302	200	102	17	9	54	245	180
October	362	156	206	40	33	56	306	205
November	233	130	103	28	6	46	185	213
December	274	162	112	11	18	47	227	255
January 1848	243	181	62	11	4	20	223	210
February 1-2	28	16	12	2	1	1	27	213**
February 3-29	270	151	119	16	11	33	237	202
March	91	52	39	7	3	8	83	172
April	111	57	54	6	2	6	105	96
May	45	28	17	1	4	1	44	62
Total***	2,421	1,406	1,015	178	99	286	1,744	–

Source: Archives of Ontario, RG 11-6, Toronto Convalescent and Fever Hospital Admission and Discharge Register, 1847–1848.

Note: Religion of the patients was not recorded until August 26, 1847; sometimes the category was left blank, with no reason offered by the secretary. Of the 2,030 patients admitted to the hospital with a denominational designation, 1,744, or 85.9%, were registered as Roman Catholic, and 286, or 14.1%, were designated Protestant.

**On February 2, 1848, there were still eight patients in the hospital who had been admitted in August 1847, and one who had been admitted in September 1847.

***At least 779 patients were recorded as having "relapsed" into illness. This means that some patients have been "double counted" in the ledger; if they relapsed and were sent to the Emigrant Hospital and then subsequently readmitted to the Convalescent Hospital. Clerks at the latter hospital offered no special designation to patients who were readmitted. A sample cross referencing of admissions to releases, using a sample size of 150 (out of the 779), reveals that perhaps little more than 25 per cent of patients who relapsed were readmitted to the Convalescent Hospital. This would allow for a margin of error in the aggregate figures (2,421) of about 195 persons or about 8 per cent of the total admissions. One can only surmise that some of the relapsed patients who did not return either died, or were released directly from the Emigrant hospital once they recovered from their illness.

The entire ledger can be viewed at www.deathorcanada.com.

Appendix C

The Famine Dead in Toronto, June 1847 to January 1848

Found in the Burial Registers of St. Paul's Parish (Roman Catholic);
St. Paul Catholic Cemetery; St. James Anglican Cemetery;
Pottersfield; *The British Colonist*

*Designates a Torontonian who died in service of the sick and infirm

W. Acton
Edward Ahern
Margaret Anderson
David Armstrong
Hugh Atkins
Robert Atkins
John Auldy
Nurse Susan Bailey*
Henry Barrett
Sally Ann Baxter
Thomas Beaty
William Bell
Margaret Bell
Alexander Berryman
Oliver Berryman
Sarah Ann Biggar
Thomas Biggar
Robert Black
Peter Blake
Thomas Boles
Jane Boles

John Bolster
Francis Booth
Mary Ann Booth
Margaret A. Bowman
Andrew Bowman
Mary Brannen
James Brennan
Elisa Brooks
Mary Brophy
Mark Brophy
Oliver Brown
William Brown
John Brown
Sarah Brown
Bridget Bryan
Michael Burke
Mary Burns
Richard Burns
Catherine Burns
Catherine Burns
Mathew Burns

Bridget Burns
Nancy Burns
Thomas Butler
Thomas Cahill
Edgens Calbraith
Rose Calgie
Pat Calgy
Pat Callaghan
Cornelius Callahan
Fanny Campbell
Robert Campbell
Johnston Campbell
David Campbell
Susan Canary
Alice Carey
Elizabeth Carey
Martin Carlow
Joseph Carroll
Thomas Carroll
Julia Carroll
Biddy Carroll

Anne Carroll
Margaret Carroll
Honora Carroll
Bridget Carwady
Pattie Casey
Catherine Casey
Catherine Casiello
Pattie Caskill
George Cass
Bessy Cassady
Rose Cassady
Patrick Cawlor
Joshua Chambers
Rachel Cherry
A Child from the
  Wharf
Pattie Clarke
Biddy Clary
Rose Clifford
James Clifford
John Cochrane
William Coke
Martin Collins
Mary Collins
Bridget Collins
William Collins
Anne Commerford
Mary Commerford
Matthew Conighan
Mary Anne Conn
Margaret Conn
Patrick Connell
Catherine Connell
John Connolly
Mary Connors
James Conolly
Mary Conroy
Anne Conroy
William Conroy
William Cook
William Cooke

John Corcoran
Mary Jane Correy
James Cosgrove
Eliza Costello
James Courtney
Michael Cowan
Jane Cox
Andrew Creagh
Johanna Creagh
Mary Ann Creagh
James Crown
James Cuff
Ann Cugheen
John Cullen
Patrick Cullin
Eliza Cummerford
Pat Cummerford
Martha Cummins
Robert Cunningham
Jane Cunningham
Sarah Cunningham
William Cunningham
Sarah Cunningham
Hugh Cunningham
Hugh Curry
Hugh Curry
Benjamin Deacon
John Deairt
Mary DeLaney
Michael Delaney
William Dempsey
James Dempsey
John Dilworth
Benjamin Dixon
Catherine Doherty*
Catherine Doherty
Bridget Doherty
James Donavan
Nelly Donavan
John Donnelly
Francis Donnelly

Michael Doohy
Margaret Doole
Owen Duffy
Mary Duffy
Edward Duffy
Michael Duffy
Sarah Duggan
Anne Dundas
John Dundas
Henry Dundas
John Dunevan
James Dunevan
P. Dunevan
Ann Dunn
Charles Dunwoodie
Arthur Dunwoody
Samuel Dunwoody
James Dunwoody
Anne Dunwoody
William Earl
Margaret Edmonds
James Edmonds
Thomas Edmunds
Robert Edwards
Margaret Elliot
James Elliott
William Evans
William Evans
Mary Fagan
Alexander Fagan
Martin Fallin
Margaret Farrell
Peggy Fitzgibbon
Margaret Flaherty
Michael Flanagan
William Fleming
Infant Fleming
Mary Flemming
Ann Flynn
Mary Foley
Mary Foley

Biddy Foulkin
Frederick Fox
Robert Fox
Frederick Fox
Janet Fox
William Fox
Frederick Fox
Mary Gahan
Ann Galbriaith
Mary Gallagher
John Gallagher
William Gallaher
Catherine Galvin
William Garrety
Nicholas Garvin
Judy Gaughan
W. Gaughan
Nelly Gelleghan
Marry Gihory
Paul Gildy
Bridget Gilhooly
William Girvin
John Glass
Michael Gleason
James Gleeson
Mary Gleeson
Mary Glover
James Gogin
John Golaghan
Anne Gorman
Catherine Gorman
Eliza Graham
Ann Graham
William Graham
James Graham
John Grant
Dr. George R. Grasett *
John Grihim
Patrick Grimes
Thomas Grindale
Mary Hagan

Margaret Hagarty
Mary Hagerty
Joseph Hamilton *
Joseph Hamilton
John Hanalan
Patrick Hanalan
Ellen Hanigan
James Hanlan
Pattie Hannan
James Hannery
Archibald Hare
Edward Harkin
Mary Harkins
William Harleton
Eliza Harleton
William Harrison *
Judy Hartegan
Biddy Haskins
Richard Hastings
Ellen Haughter
Julia Hayes
Jane Anne Heatby
Eleanor Heather
John Heatley
Thomas Heatly
Thomas Helm
Susan Henry
John Henry
Felix Henry
Joseph Henry
Felix Henry
Margaret Henry
Patrick Henry
Jane Henry
John Hickey
Peter Hickey
Patrick Hickey
Michael Higgins
Michael Higgins
Gess Higgins
Mary Anne Higgins

Betty Higgins
James Higgins
James Hinton
Betty Hirvins
Bridget Hogan
Mary Hogan
Ann Hogan
James Hogan
Ellen Hogan
Charles Hogan
Eliza Hogan
Sarah Holden
B. Howard
Michael Howard
Ellen Howard
Joseph Howe
Ellen Hoy
A Widow Hughes
Thomas H. Hunter
Benjamin Hunter
Eliza Bell Hunter
Burgess Hunter
David Alex Hunter
Burn Hutchinson
Betsy Hutchison
Arthur M. Hutton
Edward Hyland
Richard Hyland
Margaret Hyland
John Hyland
William Hyland
Patrick Hyland
Richard Hyland
Mary Hyland
Bryan Hyland
Ann Hyland
John Hyland
William Jameson
Daniel Jaucle
William Johnston
Neil Johnston

Frederick Jones
Richard Jones*
Margaret Joyce
Mary Joyce (Joice)
Richard Kearney
Martin Kearney
Simon Keeton
Rachael Kelam
Honora Kelly
James Kempston
Catherine Kennedy
Martha Kennedy
Sarah Kennedy
Mary Ann Keogh
John Kerney
John Kilpatrick
Nancy Kilpatrick
Elizabeth Kimpston
John Kinahan
Eliza Kinchin
Thomas King
Ellen King
Paul Kingston
Thomas Kingston
James Kingston
Cherry Kingston
Julia Kinney
Jane Kirkpatrick
Adam Kyle
Jane Lafferty
Thomas Lally
John Lam
W. Lambert
Julia Lane
Martha Lang
Johanna Lannigan
Catharine Lawson
David Leahy
Johannah Leary
Bessy Leary
Patrick Leary

John Leary
Mary Ann Leary
Breden Lee
Margaret Lenneghan
Catherine Lennox
Anne Jane Lettice
Mary Little
Margaret Little
Roger Longhney
Margaret Lonnery
Ellen Lorer
K.M. Lundegan
David Lynch
Mary Lyons
Flora MacDonald
Judy Machen
Hagar Machen
Mary Machen
Daniel Maddigan
Margaret Magee
Alexander Magee
Ellen Maher
Mary Mahoney
Eliza Mahoney
Anamia Martin
Bartley McAndrew
Thomas McBrien
Ann McCaffery
Anne McCaffery
John McCall
Pattie McCallin
Anne McCallum
Betty McCallum
Eliza Ann McCann
Thomas McCardle
Jane McCausland
Robert McClary
William McClelland
Eliza McClelland
James McCloy
Jane McCloy

James McCloy
Charles McCloy
Pattie McClusky
John McCormick
Mary McCormick
Catherine McCroghan
Luke McCue
Sarah McCurdy
Charles McDermot
Thomas McDonough
Margaret McDougall
John McDowell
Edward McElderry*
Mary McGee
Catharine McGee
Elizabeth McGee
Elizabeth McGee
Alexander McGee
W. McGee
Joseph McGill
Nancy McGillvray
John McGinn
Mary McGregor
Nancy McGuire
Samuel McGuire
Nancy McGuire
James McGuirren
Samuel McKay
James McKenna
James McKeogh
John McKervie
Jane McKnight
James McKron
Fields McLaughlin
Mary McLean
Mary McLellan
Mary McManus
Patrick McManus
Anne McMurray
Ann McMurray
John McNabb*

Mary McNaughton
Michael McNaulty
Flora McQuade
Hugh McTeren
John McTiernan
Catherine Mealey
Pattie Meehen
Brady Melbourne
Jane Mellon
Judy Merideth
John Middleton
Johnston Miller
Bridget Mitchell
Peggy Molloy
Thomas Monaghan
Patrick Monaghan
Martin Monahan
Bridget Monaghan
Mary Monaghan
Catherine Moone
Susan Morris
Stephen Morris
A.J. Morrison
Will Morrison
Anne Morrison
W. Morton
William Morton
Mosgrove [first name
not given]
Mary Mowbrey
James Mulholland
Ann Mullen
Ann Mullen
Sarah Mulroney
Patrick Murphy
Biddy Murphy
Catherine Murphy
James Murphy
Patrick Murphy
Benjamin Murray
Ann Murray

Anthony Murray
Mary Ann Murray
Hugh Murray
Mary Murriky
Henry Musgrove
Richard Nash
Mary Neal
Mary Neale
John Needhan
Catherine Nevin
William Newell
James Nisbet
A. Noble
Ellen Noonan
John Nowood
Mary Nunan
Mary O'Brien
Ellen O'Brien
Michael O'Bryan
Pattie O'Bryan
John O'Hara
Catherine O'Hara
Henry O'Hara
Mark O'Hara
Biddy O'Neill
Patrick O'Reiley
Peter Owens
Thomas Owens
Mary Ann Owens
William Oxley
Mary Padden
Mary Ann Paterson
Mary Ann Paterson
Richard Patten
Margaret Patterson
James Patton
Michael Patton
Margaret Peterson
Catherine Phair
Lowdon Poke
James Pollock

Robert Porter
+Bishop Michael
  Power*
Margaret Power
Mary Prendergest
John Pringle
Edward Purdey
John Purdis
Ann Quinlan
John Raley
Ellen Rawreghan
Catherine Reardon
Sarah Reed
Anne Reel
Jeremiah Regan
David Riley
James Riley
Edward Riley
John Robb
Sarah Robe
James Robey
Matthew Robinson
Catherine Robinson
Ann Robinson
John Roderick
Samuel Rodger
Michael Rodger
Bessy Rorke
Robert Roseman
James Rourke
Catherine Rourke
Harriet Rouse
John Rowe
John Runnigan
Charles Ryan
Catherine Ryan
Stephen Ryan
John Ryan
Mary Ryan
Patrick Ryan
Mary Ryan

James Ryan
John Ryan
Mary Ryan
Mary Ryan
Ann Ryan
Honora Ryan
Mary Ryan
Thomas Ryan
R. Ryan
Pat Ryland
Oliver Sage
Margaret Saple
John Scollard
Martha Scott
Mary Shanaley
Mary Shea
John Sheehan
Honora Sheehan
Michael Sheridan
Larry Sheridan
Edward Sherry
Sarah Jane Sherwood*
Mary Shewman
Thomas Sloane
Anne Slocumb*
Alice Smith
Eliza Smith
Michael Smith
Robert Smith
Ann Smith
Anne Smith
John Smith
Elizabeth Smith
Eliza Smith
Samuel Smith
Jane Smith
Margaret Smith
Honora Smith
Jane Smith

William Smith
James Smith
James Smith
Nancy Smith
John Smith
Margaret Smith
Rebecca Smith
Samuel Snaith
Sally Stinson
John Stinson
Joseph Stott
Mary Stretch
Mary Stretch
Jane Stroud
Andrew Sullivan
Daniel Sullivan
Steven Sullivan
Mary Sullivan
George Swain
Margaret Sweeny
Martin Tanney
Michael Taughy
Patrick Tehany
Margaret Temple
James Temple
Mary Thomas
John Thompson
Joseph Thompson
Joseph Thompson
John Thompson
Andrew Thompson
Catherine Tobin
John Towney
Marin Townsend
Patrick Tracy
Mary Tracy
Jane Trimble
Eliza Vance
Catherine Vance

Caroline Vance
Ellen Walch
Martin Walker
Thomas Walker
Alexander Walker
Joseph Walker
Mary Wallace
Patrick Wallace
Patrick Wallace
Peggy Wallace
Thomas Wallaron
James Wallis
John Wallis
James Wallis
Ellen Walsh
Mary Walsh
William Walsh
Michael Walsh
John Ward
Elizabeth Ward
William Waugh
Michael White
Mary Jane Whiteside
Arthur Williams
Thomas Williams
John Williamson
John Williamson
Isabella Williamson
James Williamson
Robert Willis
Robert Willis
Robert Willis
John Willis
George Wilson
James Wilson
Mary Wilson
Benjamin Wood
Mary Woods
Mary Woods

Note: The names are recorded as discovered and the spellings may vary. Several persons bore the same name, which accounts for some names repeated on the list.

❧❧

Appendix D

An Overview of the Origins and Use of St. Paul's Cemetery
Toronto, Ontario

Prepared by Mark and Patrick McGowan
Historical Consultants
September 7, 2007

Nature of the Project

This project has its origins in a meeting on Thursday, August 9, 2007, when Robert Kearns (Director of the Ireland Park Foundation Board) called a meeting at St. Michael's College that included Mr. Marc Lerman (Archivist for the Roman Catholic Archdiocese of Toronto), Nancy Carter (filmmaker), Ron Williamson (Archaeological Services Inc.) and Dr. Mark McGowan (historian). Given the recent interest in the history of Irish migration to Toronto during the Famine years (1847–1851), stimulated particularly by the opening of Ireland Park on June 21, 2007, Robert Kearns wanted to know what could be done to ascertain the actual place of burial of the 757[265] Famine dead (1847) assumed buried at St. Paul's. Although there had been an accidental discovery of remains in 1998, when workers were digging a trench for plumbing improvements at St. Paul's school, little else had been done to identify where the bodies of the Famine migrants might lie. Marc Lerman provided the archaeological assessment prepared by Historic Horizon Inc. (October 14, 1998) and a copy of the history and list of interments (1842–1857) published by the Ontario Genealogical Society. Even though it was accepted that there were still remains beneath the pavement in the St. Paul's School yard and potentially elsewhere in the vicinity of the St. Paul's rectory and the school itself, several questions were still unclear: where was the exact location of the final resting place of the Famine migrants? How extensive was the cemetery itself? How much of the original cemetery ground remained undisturbed? How may have the disturbances of recent history destroyed the integrity of the original cemetery? Given all of these questions, was it practical to undertake an archaeological survey (by sonar) of the remaining cemetery grounds?

The members present concluded with a number of suggestions. First, Marc Lerman would serve as a liaison with Archbishop Thomas Collins, who had previously expressed great interest in the project. Second, it was thought that a complete archaeological excavation of the site was neither practical nor without enormous cost. Finally, it was concluded that Dr. Mark McGowan and his assistant, Patrick McGowan, should prepare a preliminary report on the sources and manuscript evidence available on the site and report back to the group. In addition, they should prepare a short list of "filmable" items that might assist Ms. Carter and producer Craig Thompson in their preparation of the documentary tentatively titled "Summer of Sorrow" [Editor's note: now called "Death or Canada"].

Materials Available

The historical team began its work on Monday, August 13, 2007, and prepared to visit several archives, after having read the three best sources on the site: Michael Harrison, *St. Paul's Roman Catholic Parish, Burial Records, 1842–1857* (Toronto, 1996), *The Reverend E. Kelly, The Story of St. Paul's Parish, Toronto, 1822–1892* (Toronto, 1922), and John R. Triggs, *An Investigation into St. Paul's Cemetery, 80 Sackville Street, Toronto* (Toronto, 1998). The latter report was prepared when human remains were discovered on the site in 1998 by workmen who were digging a trench for pipe work near St. Paul's School. At that time, the Registrar for Cemeteries, the Toronto Catholic District School Board, and the Archdiocese of Toronto agreed to leave the site undisturbed. The task of the historical team was to explore all available manuscript records for the site and fill in as many gaps in the story as possible. The team engaged in research at the Archives of the Archdiocese of Toronto, the City of Toronto Archives, the Archives of the Congregation of the Sisters of St. Joseph, online sources, the John M. Kelly Library, and the Whitby Public Library. The team also interviewed Dr. Suzanne Scorsone, who, in 1998–99, was communications director for the Archdiocese of Toronto and one of the principal architects of the resolution regarding St. Paul's Cemetery at that time.

Early History of St. Paul's

In 1822, James Baby, a prominent French-Canadian Catholic in the town of York, reported to his bishop, Alexander Macdonell, at Kingston, that he had purchased ten acres of land south of Lot Street (Queen Street) in the eastern section of the town for £20 per acre. Baby soon reported to Macdonell that he had organized a "bee" of local Catholics, who had managed to clear five acres of the land by the end of May, that same year.[266] What Baby's correspondence proves was that the land for the church, rectory, and cemetery was held by petition (not leased) from the time of the founding of the parish. Two years later, Baby reported to the bishop that the cemetery was enclosed for the sum of £20 and the clearing and digging of the site had cost Baby, personally, an additional £12, 2 shillings and 11 pence, a sum that he had hoped the bishop would remunerate him for at his earliest convenience.[267] Between 1822 and 1826, under Baby's leadership and that of the parish trustees, local Catholics constructed a brick church building on the east side of New Street (now Power Street). This new church replaced an earlier wooden structure, and served as the only Catholic parish between Kingston and Sandwich (Windsor).[268] Little has been recorded regarding the extent of the Catholic community in York at that time, although the first recorded parish census, in 1834, indicated that St. Paul's served approximately

3,240 Catholics in York and vicinity.[269] Ten years later, the population had grown approximately 25 per cent and now totalled 4,046.[270]

The cemetery appeared to have been in continuous use from the time of its initial clearing, in 1824, until the first available records of burial in 1842. While diocesan regulations for the parish, published around 1831, mandated a formal recording of the burials in the cemetery, few records exist until the coming of Bishop Michael Power, in 1842. Given the troubles between the trustees of the parish, parishioners, and Father William O'Grady, in the early 1830s, Bishop Macdonell was explicit that all "casual revenues" for burials be recorded and be made available for the use of the church. The 24th regulation even went so far as to stipulate that "five shillings shall be paid to the Fabric [trustees] for every grave that shall be opened, except the deceased be a poor person…."[271] The regulation also indicated that the burying ground could be divided into "small relics" and "sold to individuals at such prices as the Trustees of the Ground, The Incumbant, and Church Wardens will consider reasonable."[272] Such sales re-enforce the notion that, in the early nineteenth century, families were to take responsibility for the burial of their loved ones and the maintenance of the family plot.[273] All of this data, the revenues from burials, the names of the dead, and plot sales were, by diocesan regulation 33, to be recorded in a register: "a regular rejister [sic] shall be kept in every mission of all interments, Marriages and Baptisms in the same book according to the order of their dates mentioning the day the month and the year in which the person died, his name and quality, and if a child, his age."[274] Why such registers predating 1842 do not exist is still a mystery. Either they have been lost or destroyed, or they were never undertaken at all. Father O'Grady had a long-standing battle with Bishop Macdonell, which ended with the pastor's suspension in 1833, when the parish was placed temporarily under interdict. O'Grady's successor, William Patrick McDonough, had very poor relations with parishioners, with whom he fought over money and a variety of other things.[275] Given the tempests of their times, it is conceivable that both pastors could have made the prescribed paperwork one of their lower priorities.

There are fragments, however, that provide proof of ongoing use of the cemetery at St. Paul's. In 1832, for example, slips of paper presumably filed by the Trustees indicate that it cost 2 shillings and six pence to dig a grave; coffins for the month of February required an expenditure of £5, 4 shillings and 2 pence.[276] Two years later, in 1836, John Elmsley, one of Toronto's most noted Catholic leaders and philanthropists, informed Bishop Macdonell that the sexton of the parish should expect one dollar (or 2s 6d) for every grave he digs in the summer, although it appears that few families were either willing or able to pay. According to Elmsley, "many never pay him at all, others give him a note … payable at a long date and many of these even cheat him at last." Evidently, the sexton worked for free for those Catholics who died in poverty, and charged two shillings and six pence for those who died at the local hospital. While Elmsley concluded that the sexton was paid his salary by the church "punctually," his earnings were far short of what his duties required.[277] Elmsley's comments reveal many clues to the activities at St. Paul's Cemetery prior to the keeping of registers. First, the cemetery was in use, and winter interments were more difficult than summer interments. Second, given the number of burials required by local Catholics, the sexton was grossly underpaid—suggesting both a quantity of interments and the relative poverty of the families served by the sexton. On the first clue—quantity—one might estimate interments in the mid-1830s based on the local Catholic population and comparative ratios of Catholics-to-burials, where evidence is available from the 1840s and 1850s. In 1851, the ratio of burials to Catholic population in Toronto was 2.64; in 1844, it was 3.04. If one was to take the average rate between these two years (2.84) and apply this ratio to the known population of 1834 (3,240), one could estimate that perhaps that as many as 92 persons could have been interred in the cemetery in 1834. Assuming a constant death rate of 2.84 per cent per year for the 18 unrecorded years of the cemetery, there could be well over 1,000 interments unrecorded before 1842. While the documented number of burials between 1842 and 1857 stands at 2,787,[278] at the cemetery's closure in 1857, the total interments was significantly in excess of this figure.

The second clue, relating to either the parsimony or the poverty of the Catholic community when it came to paying for burial services, may help to account for the state of neglect of the cemetery over the decades. With no evidence of "small relic" sales for some parishioners at St. Paul's, in combination with the non-payment of fees by other families in the parish, one might be able to understand why such little attention was paid to the grounds of the cemetery for so many years, even prior to the arrival of Bishop Power. Clearly, families were assumed to be taking responsibilities for the gravesites that might not necessarily be assumed by families in our own time. A family's poverty might very well explain why St. Paul's Cemetery was neglected. First, Eric Hounsom suggests that, in early York, many families could only afford wooden crosses as memorial markers,[279] which would have certainly deteriorated over time, particularly if families, for a variety of reasons, did not maintain the proverbial family plots. Even Father McDonough admitted that during his time at the parish in the late 1830s, there was a "Burying ground attached not well fenced ...."[280] One suspects from his comments that, given his modest personal revenues and his ongoing difficulties with the parishioners, he was not going to repair or rebuild the cemetery fence, something he expected was the responsibility of the parish. Given their defaulting on payments to the sexton, it appeared that St. Paul's parishioners were equally reluctant to maintain the cemetery property. If they could not share in the maintenance of their family graves, how could they possibly help maintain the entire site?

Poverty, however, is only one possible cause for the neglect. Another possible cause is the fact that immigrants to Upper Canada simply kept on moving. As David Gagan points out clearly in his scholarly demographic research on pre-Confederation Ontario, Upper Canadians were people "on the move" who frequently changed residence in search of better land, accommodations, or opportunities. This characteristic of "movement" is confirmed for urban dwellers by Michael Katz, who, in his landmark study of Hamilton, demonstrates clearly that Irish Catholic immigrants to cities were a mobile labour force.[281] If these historical trends are taken into consideration, it is little wonder that the resting places of early Catholic settlers in Toronto were quickly forgotten within a generation. Thus it was entirely possible that even if families could have maintained the graves of loved ones, they simply did not remain in York (Toronto) to do so. If Catholics were similar to the rest of the population in their peregrinations, and there is little evidence to suggest otherwise, Catholic families simply left Toronto behind, and with it a cemetery filled with friends and relations, whose resting places, it was presumed, someone else could maintain.

Despite problems of fencing and maintenance of the cemetery in the early years, there is sufficient evidence to suggest that the parish Trustees and pastor knew full well where the boundaries of the burial ground began and ended. In 1834, John Elmsley informed Bishop Macdonell that the Trustees planned to subdivide the church property that lay to the immediate south of the chapel. In a detailed map of the property that bordered New Street (Power) on the east as far as what may now be Richmond Street on the south, Elmsley and his colleagues had set aside land for a Catholic school (facing Richmond) and six lots for private homes, each having 30-foot frontage on New Street. While the land was never developed in the manner Elmsley had suggested, it did become the property that eventually became home to the first convent of the Congregation of the Sisters of St. Joseph and their House of Providence. More important is the fact that by 1834, these lands were clearly not within the confines of the cemetery, and the trustees had no intention of expanding the cemetery, which at that time lay immediately behind the chapel, west of Sackville Street and thereupon on the land running north to south adjacent to Sackville Street. Eighteen years later, in 1852, James Fitzgerald revealed to Bishop Charbonnel that these lands were still being unused and that they were "outside the present enclosed burying ground."[282] Thus, although the burial ground might have been in rough shape, contemporaries were clear about its location and its limits, suggesting that the cemetery remained undisturbed by any development in the colonial period.

The Power-Charbonnel Years: 1842–1857

With the arrival of Michael Power, the first Catholic bishop of Toronto, in June 1842, there emerges a greater clarity about the activities at St. Paul's Cemetery. Noted for his strict adherence to the Canon Law and regulations of the Church and for his eye to detail in practically all parish matters, Power quickly put Regulation 33 into practice at St. Paul's, which temporarily served as the Cathedral parish for his new diocese. During his brief episcopate (1841–1847), he made clear to all of his priests that cemeteries were sacred spaces to be properly fenced and marked by a cross at their centre, and they were not to be used "as grazing areas for livestock."[283] In October 1842, Power's Diocesan Synod passed Regulation 20, which mandated that burial registers be maintained across the diocese in both parishes and missions.[284]

As indicated previously, from the time of Power's arrival until the closing of the cemetery by Bishop Charbonnel in 1857, there were an estimated 2,787 interments. Not all of the burials were those of Irish Catholics. Of the 2,070 interments for which ethnic identity was explicit, 42.8 per cent were Irish born, 40.6 per cent Canadian, 1.2 per cent Scots and Irish, and 15 per cent "other."[285] An examination of all 2,787 burials by surname reveals a similar, yet sharper, portrait of the ethnic composition of the occupants of St. Paul's Cemetery. At least 92.2 per cent of the dead were identified as having Irish surnames, while 7.8 per cent did not.[286] The Irish clearly dominated the plots, but there were numbers of French Canadians, Scots, and English Catholics resting among them. While the Irish were clearly the majority in the community, the presence of other nationalities and origins reinforces the fact that this was a Catholic cemetery.

The Irish dominance of the cemetery, however, is not without its own set of problems. The total number of interments and the total number of Irish burials is obscured by the fact that during 1847, the most important year in terms of the volume, for the arrival of Famine migrants, some 757 names went unrecorded in the parish register. While 68 names of these Famine victims were recorded as having been buried in early 1848,[287] it still leaves the identities of possibly 689 others to chance and, once again, underestimates the number of interments in the cemetery. Accounting for why these names were not recorded in 1847 is perplexing. Power spent much of the first five months of that year in Europe, and so was not there to supervise the clergy left in charge. When he returned, the first wave of Famine refugees was arriving. By late summer, all of Power's priests were ill with typhus, a disease that Power soon contracted in late September. He died on October 1, 1847, leaving much confusion among his priests. The Catholic Church was simply overwhelmed with the sick and dying, and grossly understaffed to meet the needs of the thousands of Catholics in the Emigrant Hospital and adjoining fever sheds. The last week of August provides a typical example how the arrival of thousands of Irish Famine migrants strained the resources and energies of Toronto and its churches to the extreme. Between August 23 and 29, 233 new cases were admitted to the Emigrant Hospital, whereas only 104 patients were moved to the Convalescent Hospital. The Board of Health also recorded 71 deaths,[288] of which at least 70 per cent were Catholic and in need of burial in St. Paul's Cemetery. The ailing clergy could not manage the paperwork while daily overseeing the constant flow of interments. There is no contemporary evidence suggesting a mass burial at St. Paul's, although in his history of St. Paul's, written in 1922, Edward Kelly maintains that the Famine victims were buried in "long trenches."[289] Kelly's sources are unclear, since he did not include footnotes in his tome. The Board of Health stipulated that the graves be dug to a depth allowing for three feet of earth between the top of the coffin and the level ground, and then that the earth be heaped to a level of at least one foot above the ground.[290] While it would be difficult to follow these directives to the letter had one elected to bury the dead by use of trenches, it would not have been impossible; when the trench was completely filled, the letter of the law would have been honoured. What is clear from financial records is that some burials were recorded on the site up to December 1, 1847, when £57 17 s 3d was owed by the parish to the Board of Health for approximately 34 burials.[291]

There is no clear answer, however, to the question of where these Famine victims would have been buried. Sir Sanford Fleming's map of the area, dating from 1851, is one of the few maps that give clear boundaries to the cemetery at a time when these boundaries were clearly known and acknowledged by contemporaries. The burial ground occupied a small strip alongside the southern wall of the church—the ground immediately to the east behind the church, which joined to the principal burial area running north to south along the western side of Sackville Street.[292] The northern edge of the cemetery was approximately 163 feet to the south of Lot Street (Queen Street).[293] Fitzgerald, in his comments to Charbonnel, had indicated that this strip of land to the north of the cemetery along Queen Street required drainage, and that he knew of a man from Tipperary who was capable of the job.[294] Therefore, it is clear that there were no burials along Queen Street. This narrows down the possibilities to the area immediately adjoining the church, or the main portion of the cemetery along Sackville Street. Disturbances to this area will reveal more clues as to the final resting place of these "Famine Irish."

The vacant lands between the cemetery and New Street (Power) to the west were soon developed. In 1851, Bishop Charbonnel invited the Sisters of St. Joseph to the diocese to assist with the building of orphanages and schools. In 1854, the Sisters began occupation of the "White House"—their convent, located on the east side of Power Street, south of the Church and west of the southern edge of the cemetery.[295] They erected their own section of the cemetery for deceased sisters, which was located north of the convent but to the west of the main cemetery. Shortly thereafter, in the space adjacent (west) to the Sisters' cemetery and north of the convent along Power Street, the Sisters commenced construction on the House of Providence, which opened in 1857.[296] The property upon which all of these structures were built had been the surplus lands indicated by Elmsley in 1834 and Fitzgerald in 1852. The boundaries of the cemetery for St. Paul's would have been clearly understood and avoided by these newer structures. Although Charbonnel formally closed St. Paul's Cemetery in 1857, directing all further burials to the new St. Michael's Cemetery (1855) on Yonge Street, the Sisters maintained their portion of the cemetery until May 14, 1879, when the remains of 27 sisters were exhumed and removed to St. Michael's Cemetery.[297] The Sisters' cemetery had been moved in order to make way for a new chapel, situated to the east of the House of Providence. It was dedicated by Archbishop John Joseph Lynch on the Feast of the Epiphany, January 6, 1882.[298]

Disturbances

It appears that so long as the boundaries and monuments of the old St. Paul's Cemetery remained intact in living memory, the integrity of the cemetery would be preserved. About ten years after its closing, local Catholic citizens expressed their concerns about the lack of maintenance and care given the old burial ground. Responding to the levelling or removal of the broken and poorly maintained tombstones, by order of Archbishop Lynch, Catholic petitioners made specific demands for the rededication of the burial ground:

> We, the undersigned Catholics of the City of Toronto, who have resided in Toronto for upward of 30 years, have recently learned that, with the exception of three, all the graves in the Burial ground attached to St. Paul's Church of this City, have been levelled down, and the monument formerly erected by the friends of some of those buried there, removed from their respective places. So that, with the three exceptions referred to, no indication remains of the place having been a burial ground or … whether the same was ever marked out by monument or not.[299]

There was hope that the Archbishop would promote the building of a monument to commemorate the cemetery, but nothing was done immediately in the wake of the petition. Nevertheless, the petition suggests that even the petitioners were so detached from the cemetery that they only learned of the removal of the monuments after the fact. Moreover, with only three monuments remaining intact, the memory of the burial ground would survive only so long as these markers remained in place and there was common recognition that a cemetery had been in that location along Sackville Street. One might say this living memory was still intact in 1879, when the Sisters of St. Joseph were careful not to disturb the remains in their portion of the cemetery, prior to the construction of the chapel wing to the House of Providence. Thereafter, other disturbances occurred, suggesting that there was far less knowledge of what lay in the empty lots to the east of the buildings that sat on Power Street.

In 1887, ground was broken on a new St. Paul's Church (the present basilica) on lands at the corner of Queen and Power—ground that had never been part of the cemetery.[300] The new Church was immediately to the north of the old St. Paul's Church, which was used as a parish hall until Archbishop Denis O'Connor ordered its demolition in 1903. On the site of old St. Paul's and its little chapel of St. Anne, which had been erected in 1874 as a small "winter chapel" adjoining the old church, the parish built a new rectory for the resident clergy. According to Kelly, "nor were there any bodies found beneath it."[301] The new construction had not disturbed the burial ground. Nor, evidently, did the building of St. Vincent's Infant Home (later, Mercy Hospital for the Incurables) in 1906, to the east of the House of Providence, but south of the old burial ground.[302] In fact, in that same year, 1906, local historian John Ross Robertson acknowledged the location of the burial ground in the fifth volume of the popular *Landmarks of Toronto* series.[303] Thus, there is evidence that some "locals" still possessed lingering memory or inherited memory of where the old burial ground had been three to four decades after its closing. Even Kelly's admission, in 1922 that there were no "bodies found" indicates that, as a local priest, he was aware of a burial ground close by.

Ten years later, however, this shadowy recollection of the burial ground may have dissipated completely, at least until the events of February 1932. The Sisters had plans to expand the facilities of Mercy Hospital for the Incurables, which had its entrance on Sackville Street, but was south of the old burial ground. The new plans called for an annex to the north of the building (eventually Bosco Hall), which would serve as a dining room for the men and women of the hospital and whose basement "would be excavated throughout its length."[304] Our map work, which included drawing a scale version based on the maps provided by Dr. Triggs's report and a map provided by the Sisters of St. Joseph, indicates clearly that the annex wing of Bosco Hall was built on the southern portion of the old burial ground. While neither the Sisters nor the local press reported the exhumation of human remains during its construction, it is difficult to believe that given its location, human remains were not found. Perhaps the discretion of the Sisters and local Catholics prevented the word of such a macabre study from getting out. One interesting coincidence to the excavation of Bosco Hall is the dedication of a monument to Bishop Power and the Famine migrants in October later that year. On Sunday, October 9, 1932, at the conclusion of the annual parade of the Holy Name Society, a crowd of 25,000 society members paraded from Queen's Park to St. Paul's, where they were met by Archbishop Neil McNeil of Toronto, Archbishop Thomas O'Donnell of Halifax (a former Irish-born priest of the Diocese of Toronto), Ontario Chief Justice William Mullock, and Canadian Chief Justice F.J. Latchford. Mass was celebrated and O'Donnell offered an eloquent homily eulogizing Bishop Power, "a martyr to priestly duty," and the Irish migrants who were victims in the "pest house sheds" and whose "ashes" lay "buried in adjacent ground."[305] The memorial itself consisted of a stone base, with a bronze portrait of Power, and a large bronze Pietà, cast by the DaPrato Statuary Company of Montréal. Dean John Laurence Hand commissioned the work for $4,112 as a memento of his 50th anniversary of ordination (a jubilee he would celebrate on November 1).[306] The entire episode raises many questions: why had the city waited until 1932 to memorialize Power and the old burial ground? Had the burial ground, or at least its physical extent, really been forgotten? Had something been unearthed during the excavation at Bosco Hall that prompted this memorialization? The year 1932 marks no particular anniversary for either the Famine or Michael Power. Did Dean Hand use his anniversary as a means to mark the jarring discoveries at Bosco Hall? The coincidence of the building of Bosco Hall and the unveiling of the Famine memorial within seven months of each other deepen the mystery about how much was known about St. Paul's Cemetery and its size nearly 75 years after its closing and 65 years after the removal of most of its monuments.

The building of Bosco Hall also raises questions about the remains of the Famine Irish. Had the cemetery been filling immediately adjacent to the old church and directly to the east of it (as is suggested by the uncovering of four or more individual vaults in 1998), it is possible that burials in the late 1840s fanned out to the extremities of the cemetery. In this case, the most likely resting place for the Famine Irish would be the areas in the southeast section of the cemetery, or the location of Bosco Hall. This mystery may never be solved, since the House of Providence, Mercy Hospital, and all of the "physical plant buildings" (boiler house and laundry) were sold to the City of Toronto in 1963.[307] Within a year, the entire site that had once been Catholic Toronto's nerve centre of social services was covered in fill, in preparation for the building of the Richmond Street off-ramp for the Don Valley Parkway.[308]

The most noteworthy disturbance of the burial ground came, however, in 1959, when workmen preparing the foundation for the new St. Paul's School unearthed numerous bones and fragments of caskets. Prior to 1959, St. Paul's School had been standing on the south side of Queen Street, at the corner of Queen and Sackville. This was the same piece of property described by Fitzgerald in 1852 as needing drainage. In early 1959, the Archdiocese sold land south of the old school to the Toronto Catholic Separate School Board for one dollar. The parcel of land was substantial, consisting of a northern boundary running from Sackville Street, west to St. Paul's Church (new), a distance of 229 feet four inches, south along Sackville Street for 122 feet, and a southern boundary that proceeded west from Sackville Street a distance of 227 feet, five inches. The entire parcel of land was located 163 feet, 15 3/4 inches south from Queen Street.[309] In other words, the Archdiocese had sold much of the original burial ground to the school board. Later that year, in May, workers excavating the new school discovered human remains. Work stopped, but only temporarily. In a statement written for Cardinal James McGuigan, the archdiocesan lawyer, Arthur Kelly, explained that the records of the Archdiocese could not verify a "definable area which can be distinguished as cemetery lands," and that the recent discovery of remains appeared to be evidence of "unplanned, sporadic and casual burials of which there is no record."[310] McGuigan reported this opinion to the Ontario Minister of Health, Matthew B. Dymond, and added that the remains would be removed and re-interred. The Minister acknowledged the letter by the end of June and the case appeared to be closed.[311]

The remains were placed in three, perhaps four, caskets, and transported for reburial at Mount Hope Catholic Cemetery. Each casket contained "multiple bones from an unknown number of those originally buried at St. Paul's." The fourth casket, which apparently had been filled with children's bones, could not be accounted for when, in 1998, construction work outside St. Paul's school unearthed more human remains. Each of the three known caskets was placed in separate graves in several sections of the cemetery (Section 9, grave 51, range 44; section 18, grave 40, range 15; section 18, grave 111, range 35). Each grave had ample room for an additional casket, if necessary, but none of the three graves bore a monument of any kind. The Catholic press and secular press made no mention of the bones having been excavated.

In 1963, when a new rectory was under construction in an area that would have been a portion of the burial ground immediately to the rear of the "old church," evidence of more disturbance to the site was encountered. This time, the parish priest, Father W. O'Brien, reported to Bishop Philip Pocock that the workmen were having a difficult time laying the foundations for the rectory because the sub soil was littered with fill from the old church, which had been demolished in 1903.[312] Later, in the 1980s, when renovations were undertaken to the eastern side of the rectory, there were stories afoot that some human remains had been discovered. It is possible that the demolition of the old church may not have uncovered bodies, but it certainly disturbed the burial ground by the haphazard ploughing under of bricks, wood, and stone, as workers managed a simple way of discarding some of the ruins of the old church. This fill would have placed yet another layer of materials over part of the burial ground (the part resembling a panhandle on

Fleming's map).

The site was disturbed once again in 1998, when workers at the north side of St. Paul's School were digging a trench for drainage pipes. Amidst significant publicity, the Toronto Catholic District School Board, in compliance with Section 70 of the Ontario Cemeteries Act and in consultation with the Archdiocese of Toronto, hired the archaeological firm of Historic Horizon Inc. to investigate the area of the school playground where the trench had breached the burial ground. On September 28 to 30, 1998, the archaeological team investigated six "individual burials" that were located approximately 0.75 to 1.23 metres below the asphalt. Each grave contained human remains and all but one showed evidence of coffin material. Moreover, these were not evidence of "mass burial."[313] The remains were reburied on the site and, after significant discussions between the school board, archdiocese, and registrar for cemeteries, it was agreed to leave the site undisturbed. It was also suggested at the time that a memorial plaque be affixed to the east wall of the church building to identify the existence of an old Catholic cemetery on the school grounds. Archdiocesan officials quite rightly wanted any memorial to acknowledge both the Irish and Catholics of other ethnicities who were buried on what was historically considered "a Catholic burial ground" without reference to any specific ethnicity. Later, Action Grosse Île erected a modest plaque on the north wall of the school, overlooking the trench, which commemorated the Irish presence in the burial ground.

Conclusions

Having weighed as much evidence as was made available to us, this historical team makes the following observations:

1. There was continuous use of the St. Paul's Burial ground from 1822 to 1857, and the number of interments far exceeded the 2,787 that were recorded. In 1959, Arthur Kelly and Cardinal McGuigan were incorrect in their assessment that these burials were "unplanned, sporadic, and casual." The documentary evidence strongly gainsays this assessment. The living memory of the cemetery seems hazy

by 1900. If it existed at all, by the 1930s it was either "inherited memory" or a new set of memories jarred by the possibility of what was unearthed when excavating Bosco Hall.

2. There is no way of knowing for certain where the Irish Famine victims are currently resting, although it is reasonable to hypothesize that their resting place is less likely under the existing school yard than in areas that have been disturbed by other ventures. The Historic Horizon report of 1998 makes clear that the sample burial vaults uncovered were evidence of single grave burials at the periphery of the original cemetery. If it is assumed that, due to volume and the necessity to bury typhus victims quickly, which was the order of the day in 1847, trenches would have been more effective and certainly in keeping with the letter of the Board of Health Regulations at that time. If Kelly was correct, therefore, these graves do not represent the hasty nature of burial required by circumstances in 1847.

3. It is reasonable to hypothesize that, if St. Paul's was similar to other burial grounds in the vicinity of a church (St. James, Colgan, for instance), burials tended to radiate "out" from the church building. In the case of St. Paul's, with interments dating from the early 1820s, it is not impossible to imagine that burials in 1847 would be in the peripheral areas of the cemetery, perhaps the southeastern section of the cemetery. If this be the case, those remains would have been disturbed first, not by the Richmond Street ramp, but by the excavation for Bosco Hall in 1932. We believe that this part of the cemetery was already disturbed, only to be made worse by the addition of tons of fill for the DVP ramps in 1964. Thus, any attempt to excavate this area would be costly, disruptive to traffic, and, in the end, futile.

4. There are now two memorials on or near the site—one at the corner of Queen and Power (1932), and the plaque on St. Paul's School. There are no memorials to the dead resting in three separate graves in Mount Hope Cemetery. Since these are bodies exhumed in haste, willy-nilly, in 1959, and since these remains were described

by Archdiocesan officials as "unplanned, sporadic, and casual," it is plausible that some of these remains might date from 1847. The section of the burial ground upon which the school sits would have been part of the periphery stated above in #3. This being the case, we recommend that if any commemoration is to take place, it should be a correction to the oversight committed in 1959: to recognize the three relocated graves at Mount Hope Cemetery.

Appendix E

The Ireland Park Foundation

Mark McGowan with Robert Kearns

Ireland Park, Toronto

The Ireland Park Foundation Famine Memorial is located at the southeast corner of Bathurst Quay, now renamed Eireann Quay by the City of Toronto in honour of the opening of Ireland Park in June 2007.

Ireland Park is boundaried to the north by the empty grain silos of the Canada Malting Company and to the south and east by Lake Ontario, which forms the channel to the Toronto Island Airport. The founder of Ireland Park Foundation, Robert G. Kearns, was inspired by the bronze sculptures on Custom House Quay in Ireland. Created by Irish sculptor Rowan Gillespie, they were donated to the city of Dublin by the Smurfit Foundation in 1997. The seven bronze sculptures depict the "Departure" of Irish Famine emigrants from the ravages of hunger and fever in their homeland bound for ships heading for Canada and the United States. Promotional material for Ireland Park, Toronto, describes the Dublin sculptures as "powerfully evocative and beautifully resolved artistically. They depict starvation and destitution with a gritty clarity." Ireland Park, Toronto, provided the opportunity to complement the Dublin "Departure" with a Canadian "Arrival."

Following three years of private lobbying by Robert G. Kearns, the City of Toronto adopted a motion tabled at Council by Councillor Olivia Chow in July 2000 to donate land for the creation of an Irish Famine memorial park on Toronto's waterfront. Kearns, an Irish-born entrepreneur with a keen interest in history, gathered together a team of scholars, business people, public servants, artists, and interested citizens of Irish birth and descent to plan for a memorial to the Great Famine migration to British North America. This group became incorporated as Ireland Park Foundation in the Spring of 2000.

The Ireland Park site, measuring 45 metres by 25 metres, would have been underwater in Toronto Harbour in 1847, the year with the highest number of arrivals from Ireland. Today, it is within the sightlines of what would have been Dr. Rees's Wharf and in close proximity to Widows and Orphans Asylum and the Convalescent Hospital, both of which were built as a direct result of the Famine migration.

Key to the development of Ireland Park was Jonathan M. Kearns (Principal, Kearns-Mancini Architects Inc.), Robert's brother. Jonathan, a noted Toronto architect, was responsible for the overall design of the Park, especially the stonework, the sculptural limestone wall, and the glass tower. Rowan Gillespie created five life-size bronze figures depicting famine emigrants arriving on the Toronto waterfront; they stand at the eastern end of the park. In 1998, the artist visited Toronto and envisioned at least four sculptures for the site, later to become five. Several of the sculptures in the group depict the sorrow, horror, and pathos that was the Famine and the process of migration from Ireland in 1847. These include an emaciated youth, referred to as "The Orphan Boy," another figure referred to as "The Apprehensive Man," and a female figure in the last moments of life lying on the ground. Two other sculptures—a man standing with arms uplifted, referred to as "The Jubilant Man" (cast in the image of Gillespie's great-great-grandfather, who made the journey in 1847 to Canada), and "The Pregnant Woman"— are symbolic of the migrants' hope for a new beginning in Canada. The gaunt and, to some, haunting figures look out onto Toronto Harbour and the modern city skyline from the shadow of the empty grain towers, an ironic juxtaposition given the nature of this commemoration. Each figure was donated through the generosity of local benefactors.[314]

The second notable element of the Park is an imposing 5-metre-high wall of Kilkenny limestone, 400 tons of which were brought from Ireland. The stone was supplied by Feeley Limestone, a family-run business that has been quarrying limestone in Ireland since 1793. The wall provides a boundary to the west end of the Park. The sculptural wall and the flooring upon which it stands invoke the feeling of a rough, harsh, rocky landscape in the west of Ireland, from whence so many of Toronto's Irish Famine migrants came. From the eastern end of the Park, the wall is seen to be divided into fourteen individual columns of Irish limestone. The wall is sliced apart at regular intervals, forming the columns; within the gaps are engraved the names of the identified Famine dead in Toronto. At night, these names and the sculptures are washed with light to a design created by electrical engineer Tony McDonnell.

The stonework in Ireland Park was beautifully laid by Trinity Custom Masonry, a team of craftsmen led by Fergus Tyrrell, Finbarr Sheehan, and David Underwood. Construction of the park was managed by Kenaidan Contracting, led by Aiden Flatly. Also standing in the park are a group of red oak trees, indigenous to both Ireland and Canada.

Credit: E.E. McGowan

Orphan Boy and Commemoration Wall

The "soft" landscaping was installed by Cthal Boyd of Shamrock Landscaping to a design by landscape architect John Quinn. Structural engineering services were provided by Scott Wallace of Read Jones Christoffersen and Mike Picco of Picco Engineering.

In 2005, Ireland Park Foundation engaged and helped to fund a research project to investigate the circumstances surrounding the arrival of the Irish Famine emigrants in Toronto from public and private archival sources. This research team was led by Mark McGowan, a full professor in the History department of the University of Toronto, and Principal of St. Michael's College. McGowan is also associated with Ireland Park as historical advisor to the Foundation Board. By means of cemetery ledgers, newspapers, and manuscript collections, McGowan, Michael Chard, Patrick McGowan, and Neil Sands were able to recover over 660 names of men, women, and children who died either in the fever hospital or elsewhere in the city. Their mandate from Ireland Park Foundation was to attempt to restore to memory the lost names of the 1,124 Famine dead in Toronto and to compile as complete an account as possible of the events that took place in the city in the summer of 1847.

The discoveries of the research team included the fact that almost 30 per cent of the dead were Protestants or members of the Church of England. To this end, Ireland Park Foundation prepared a special memorial stone for St. James Cemetery, Toronto, the site of at least 281 Protestant and Anglican burials of Famine and fever victims in 1847. On the morning of June 21, 2007, prior to the dedication of the Park, Irish President Mary McAleese, Toronto's Anglican Archbishop Terence Finlay, and Toronto's Roman Catholic Archbishop Thomas Collins dedicated the memorial at St. James Cemetery, marking the first known Famine memorial in the world exclusively dedicated to Protestant and Anglican dead. Ireland Park Foundation also commissioned a one-of-a-kind hand-tooled leather-bound volume containing all the names of the Famine dead that have been recovered by the research team. This record of Toronto's lost Famine dead was presented to President McAleese by Robert G. Kearns at the park opening ceremony to represent the return of their identity to the people of Ireland.

In September 2007, in an effort to track down the final resting places of the Catholic majority of Famine migrants, Ireland Park Foundation asked Mark McGowan and Patrick McGowan to examine the origins

Credit: Ballinran Productions

Photo of the wall and the name John Willis

and evolution of the St. Paul's burial ground; the results of that exploration are found in Appendix D of this book. Because of a paucity of Catholic burial ledgers for the year 1847, fewer Catholic names appear on the list of the dead (see Appendix C) and on the memorial wall itself. Thus, despite the fact that Catholic Irish made up over 70 per cent of the dead in Toronto in 1847, they are under-represented on the monument because of the loss, destruction, or non-existence of burial records. It is possible that the sheer numbers of dead overwhelmed the local cadre of priests, most of whom were knocked out of action, having contracted typhus or "the ships' fever." Moreover, perhaps because of the high numbers of potential Irish speakers among migrants from the west of Ireland, it is also possible that local non-Irish–speaking orderlies, doctors, and clergy could not decipher Irish names due to their heavily accented English. Also, many patients were too weak to speak clearly or audibly if asked their name. This situation may account for the wide variations in spellings of the surnames of the known dead (see Appendix C).

Finally, also included among the wall's names of the Famine and fever dead are the names of eleven Torontonians who sacrificed their lives in the service of their fellow human beings. Among them are Dr. George Grasett, chief medical officer of the Emigrant Hospital; The Right Reverend Michael Power, Roman Catholic bishop of Toronto; Susan Bailey, nurse; and Edward McElderry, Emigration Agent for Toronto.

The third outstanding element in the Park is a column that is illuminated at night by a shaft of light emitted from a tower of glass bricks. Lighting was produced by Chris Nelson of Nelson & Garrett Custom Lighting, Toronto. The column contains three computer terminals that provide the visiting public with information about the site and the history of the Irish Famine migration to Toronto. Each brick in the column came as the result of donations from the general public—both individuals and community organizations.[315] Literature for the Park refers to the illuminated tower as "symbolic as a beacon both of the 'new world' and the hopefulness for the future of the arriving emigrants." In some ways, this intention reflects the Foundation's guiding principles to preserve the memory of the Famine, to acknowledge and celebrate the contribution of the Irish to Canadian society, and to "reinforce the Canadian traditions of welcoming waves of immigrants from around the world."

Associated with the Park and with the production of the docudrama *Death or Canada* by Ballinran Films (Canada) and Tile Films (Ireland) was the opportunity to excavate the site of the Emigrant Hospital and fever sheds at the corner of King and John Streets in Toronto's downtown core, soon to be the site of the headquarters of the Toronto Film Festival. The window of time was narrow for an investigation of what artifacts and ruins might lie beneath what had been a nondescript parking lot adjoining a local tavern. In autumn 2006, Dr. Ronald F. Williamson and his team from Archaeological Services Incorporated began an exploratory dig of the site. His team discovered part of the foundation of the old hospital and several artifacts, including pieces of clay pipes, part of a gun, crockery, remnants of a delousing comb, and

Credit: Archaeological Services Inc./ Ballinran Productions

Ariel photo of dig at King and John Streets, Toronto, 2006

Facsimile of the harp brooch

a harp brooch. The brooch became the subject of much discussion, perhaps the remnant of a symbol worn by a migrant, or a cap badge from a local member of an Irish-inspired military or militia unit. Producers of the film *Death or Canada* had a replica of the brooch made for their docudrama. It became a recurring theme, and was worn by an immigrant, John Willis, through the dramatic sequences of the film. This little icon became an imaginative link symbolizing the migration from Ireland to Canada.

On June 20 and 21, 2007, several festivities and commemorations took place around the opening of the Park. The evening of June 20 featured a concert at Roy Thomson Hall in Toronto. Entitled "The Arrival," it was headlined by Canadian musical artist Loreena McKennitt, who is also a member of the Park board. The evening also included the premiere Canadian performance of Patrick Cassidy's "Famine Remembrance Symphony" by the Elora Festival Singers, conducted by Noel Edison. The Irish poet John O'Donnell and the Celtic Tenors also performed.

The next day, President Mary McAleese of the Republic of Ireland (and patron of the Park) and the Most Reverend Thomas Collins, Roman Catholic Archbishop of Toronto, attended a blessing and children's concert at St. Paul's Roman Catholic elementary school, which

Credit: Ballinran Productions

was built on the site of the Famine burial ground and the city's first Catholic cemetery. The ceremony was followed by the aforementioned blessing and dedication at St. James Cemetery. Later that day, adjacent to Ireland Park, but at Norway Park (which could hold a large crowd), Ireland Park was formally opened and dedicated by President Mary McAleese. In attendance on the stage were the Right Honourable Dalton McGuinty, Premier of Ontario, himself a descendant of Irish immigrants to the Ottawa Valley; Federal Finance Minister Jim Flaherty, who takes great pride in his Galway roots and whose government granted $500,000 to the Park; Toronto Mayor David Miller; the Anglican Bishop of Toronto, Terrence Finlay; the Roman Catholic Archbishop of Toronto, Thomas Collins; the Irish Ambassador to Canada, Declan Kelly, and his wife, Anne; and Park Chairman Robert G. Kearns. The event was attended by over 3,000 local citizens of Irish birth and descent, as well as many visitors from Ireland.

This event – one of the city's largest Irish public gatherings – involved months of preparatory work by a special team from the board of Ireland Park Foundation. This team was led by Oliver Murray and included John Maxwell, Terry Smith, Ken Tracey, and Colum Bastable. The Park was also graced with the presence of the *L.E. Eithne*, the flagship of the Irish Naval Service, which moored alongside the quay at Ireland Park. Following the ceremony, the Park welcomed its first visitors. It has had countless visitors since.

Credit: Ireland Park Foundation

Irish President Mary McAleese opens Ireland Park. The Hon. Jim Flaherty (left) and Toronto mayor David Miller (right) look on.

145

Endnotes

[1] Donald H. Akenson, *The Irish in Ontario* (Kingston: McGill-Queen's University Press, 1984).

[2] Christopher Morash, *Writing the Irish Famine* (Oxford: Clarendon Press, 1995); Cathal Poirteir, "Folk Memory and the Famine," in Poirteir, ed., *The Great Irish Famine* (Dublin: Mercier Press, 1995), 219–31.

[3] S.H. Cousens, "The Regional Pattern of Emigration During the Great Irish Famine, 1846–1851," *Institute of British Geographers, Transactions and Papers* 28 (1960): 119; and Cousens, "The Reginal Variation in Mortality During the Great Irish Famine," *Proceedings of the Royal Irish Academy*, Vol. 63, section C, no. 3 (1963): 127.

[4] Library and Archives Canada (hereafter LAC), Colonial Office, 384/82, Colonial Land and Emigration Commission, Eighth General Report, (June 1848), 15–17 and 33. Reel 1746, frame 166–8 and 175. See Appendix 1 for migration statistics. Cecil Houston and William Smyth, *Irish Emigration and Canadian Settlement: Patterns, Links, and Letters* (Toronto: University of Toronto Press, 1990) provides an excellent overview of Irish migration to Canada. Akenson, *The Irish in Ontario*, 29–32.

[5] Gearóid Ó Tuathaigh, *Ireland Before the Famine, 1798–1848* (Dublin: Gill and Macmillan, 1972, 2007 ed.), 116.

[6] Cousens, "Regional Variation in Mortality,"128.

[7] Liam Kennedy, Paul S. Ell, E.M. Crawford and L.A Clarkson, *Mapping the Great Irish Famine* (Dublin: Four Courts Press, 1999), Figure I, 26; Mary Daly, *The Famine in Ireland* (Dundalk: Historical Association of Ireland, 1986), 2 and 18.

[8] Ó Tuathaigh, *Ireland Before the Famine*, 1798–1848, 121.

[9] Kevin Whelan, "Pre and Post-Famine Landscape Change," in Poirtier, *The Great Famine*, 21: Cousens, "Regional Pattern of Emigration,"125; Christine Kinealy, *This Great Calamity: The Irish Famine 1845–52* (Dublin: Gill and Macmillan,1994), 5.

[10] *Globe*, 19 August 1845.

[11] Robert Morgan, *Early Cape Breton: From Founding to Famine*, 1784–1851 (Sydney: Breton Books, 2000), 136–52.

[12] E. Margaret Crawford, "Food and Famine," in Poirtier, *The Great Famine*, 63;

[13] Cormac O'Grada, *The Great Irish Famine* (Dublin, 1989), 76.

[14] It should be noted that the crop of potatoes did not fail in autumn 1847, but this

was too late for the tens of thousands suffering from hunger and a variety of illnesses. Crops failed again in the following year.

[15] Trevelyan served directly under the Chancellor of the Exchequer, Sir Charles Wood.

[16] Peter Gray, "Ideology and the Famine," in Poirtier, The Great Famine, 89–90; Kinealy indicates that the programs began in August 1846 and were numerous in the West of Ireland. Kinealy, This Great Calamity, 58–59; Peter Gray, The Irish Famine (New York: Harry N. Abrams, 1995), 47.

[17] Cited in Matthew Stout, "The Geography and Implications of the Post-Famine Population Decline in Baltyboys, County Wicklow," in Chris Morash and Richard Hayes, eds., 'Fearful Realities': New Perspectives on the Famine (Dublin: Irish Academic Press, 1996), 24–25.

[18] James S. Donnelly, "'Irish Property Must Pay for Irish Poverty': British Public Opinion and the Great Irish Famine," in Morash and Hayes, 'Fearful Realities,' 60. William Gregory was the Conservative Member of Parliament for Dublin City and a landlord in County Galway. His amendments came in response to the proposed extension of the Poor Law to include massive outdoor relief to be paid for by Irish landlords.

[19] Kinealy, Great Calamity, 180–1.

[20] In Stout, "Geography and Implications," 28.

[21] Stout, "Geography and Implications," 31.

[22] Gray, "Ideology," 91; James Donnelly, "Mass Eviction and the Great Famine: The Clearance Revisited," in Poirtier, The Great Famine, 171.

[23] Punch (1847), Bound Collection, 91.

[24] Punch (1847), Bound Collection, 183.

[25] Donnelly, "Irish Property," 61–62.

[26] Daly, The Famine, 29.

[27] Limerick Reporter, 19 January 1847.

[28] Limerick Reporter, 12 February 1847.

[29] Limerick Reporter, 5 February 1847.

[30] Limerick Chronicle, 29 May 1847

[31] Limerick Reporter, 23 February 1847 and 9 March 1847.

[32] Cited in Peter Foynes, The Great Famine in Skibbereen (Skibbereen: Irish Famine Commemoration Ltd., 2004), 52

[33] Foynes, The Great Famine in Skibbereen, 85.

[34] Limerick Reporter, 23 February 1847 and 9 March 1847.

[35] Kevin H Murphy, Echoes of Caher (Killarney: Killarney Printing, 1999), 46.

[36] LAC, MG 24 I, Vol. 22, Patrick Knowlan Papers, John Nowlan to Patrick Nowlan, 30 September 1847.

[37] Crawford, "Food and Famine," 64; Kinealy, Great Calamity, 47–48.

[38] Daly, The Famine, 57; Kinealy, 86.

[39] Cited in Famine Ireland: Limerick. Extracts from the British Parliamentary Papers, 1846–1849, Relevant to Limerick City and County, Vol. 2, Board of Works, S.W. Roberts, Drainage Commission Office, Castlebellingham to Poor Relief Department, 5 February 1847, 69.

[40] Board of Works, Famine Ireland, "Table Showing the Number of Persons Employed," 69.

[41] Board of Works, Famine Ireland, Appendix F, "A Schedule showing the Names of

persons injured, Nature of the Injury, Date of Occurrence, where Committed, the Officer by whom reported, with consequent Local Results," 60–61 and 66.

[42] Board of Works, *Famine Ireland*, "Extract from Report of Lieutenant Miller, Inspecting Officer, County Tipperary, N.R., for the week ending 9 January 1847," 103.

[43] Amartya Sen, *Development as Freedom* (New York: Anchor Books, 1999), 168–70.

[44] Daly, *The Famine*, 88.

[45] Sean Kierse, *The Famine Years in the Parish of Killaloe, 1845–1851* (Killaloe: Boru Books, 1984), 29.

[46] Christine Kinealy, *This Great Calamity*.

[47] Michael D'Arcy Ryan, "Commissioners, Guardians and Paupers: Life and Death in the Limerick Poor Law Union, 1838–1850 (Ph.D. Dissertation, Concordia University, 2005), 153–66.

[48] Colleen M. Towns, "Relief and Order: The Public Response to the 1847 Famine Irish Migration to Upper Canada," (MA Thesis, Queen's University, Kingston, 1990), 13.

[49] *Famine Ireland … Extracts*, Vol. I, Mr. Erichsen to George Trevelyan, 13 February 1847, 126; Mary Daly, "The Great Famine and Irish Society," in Cecil Houston and Joseph Leydon, eds., *Ireland: The Haunted Ark* (Toronto: Celtic Arts, 1996), 6.

[50] *Limerick Reporter*, 8 January 1847.

[51] Cousens, Regional Variation in Mortality," 132.

[52] *Limerick Reporter*, 8 January 1847.

[53] Crawford, 67.

[54] *Limerick Chronicle*, 3 March and 24 February 1847. *Limerick Reporter*, 19 January 1847. Frank M. Prendergast, *St. Michael's Parish, Limerick: Its Life and Times* (Limerick: [the parish], c2000), 4.

[55] *Limerick Reporter*, 19 January 1847; Kevin Hannan, "The Famine in Limerick," *The Old Limerick Journal: Famine Edition* no. 32 (Winter 1995), 21. In 1847, 2,204 people were served in Limerick under the new legislation.

[56] Kennedy et al., *Mapping the Great Irish Famine*, 16–17 and 38.

[57] *Limerick Chronicle*, 15 May 1847.

[58] *Limerick Chronicle*, 12 May 1847.

[59] *Limerick Chronicle*, 12 May 1847.

[60] *Limerick Chronicle*, 12 May 1847. Also see Cousens, "Regional Pattern of Emigration," 128, which indicates an inverse relationship between migration and pauperism, except in County Mayo.

[61] *Limerick Reporter*, 4 May 1847.

[62] *Limerick Chronicle*, 12 May 1847.

[63] *Limerick Chronicle*, 24 April 1847.

[64] *Limerick Chronicle*, 31 March 1847.

[65] *Limerick Chronicle*, 24 March 1847.

[66] *Limerick Chronicle*, 22 May 1847.

[67] LAC, Colonial Office, 384/82, Colonial Land and Emigration Commission, Eighth General Report, (June 1848):15–17. See Appendix A.

[68] British Parliamentary Papers, Volume 17, Sessions, 1847–48, Report of A.C. Buchanan, 31 March 1848, pp. 471–7.

[69] Robert Grace, "Irish Immigration and Settlement in a Catholic City, 1842–61," *Canadian Historical Review* 84 (June 2003): 240.

[70] LAC, Colonial Office Papers, 384/80, "Guide for Emigrants to British North America," March 1847, 197.

[71] The 36 non-British ships came from German ports. BPP, Vol 17, Buchanan Report.

[72] BPP, Vol. 17, Buchanan Report. And Andre Charbonneau & Andre Sevigny, *1847 Grosse Île: A Record of Daily Events* (Ottawa: Canadian Heritage, Parks Canada, 1997), 21.

[73] Kennedy et al. note 40 per cent depletion rates in the populations of Galway, Clare, Tipperary, Limerick, and Kerry between 1851 and 1861, suggesting that the patterns noted in 1847 appeared to continue significantly over the next decade. *The Great Irish Famine*, Map 12, 41. *Limerick Chronicle*, 14 April 1847, confirms that the majority of the emigrants come from Limerick, Clare, and Tipperary.

[74] Kierse, *The Famine Years in the Parish of Killaloe*, 1, 62 and 64.

[75] Peter Gray, *The Irish Famine*, 94; see table.

[76] O'Gallagher, *Eyewitness*, Table 8, 352.

[77] National Famine Museum, Strokestown Park, County Roscommon, Gallery 7. Stephen J Campbell, *The Great Irish Famine: Words and Images from the Famine Museum, Strokestown Park, County Roscommon* (NP: The Famine Museum, 1994), 48.

[78] Gray, *The Irish Famine*, 94; see table.

[79] Marianna O'Gallagher, *Grosse Île: Gateway to Canada*; Archives of the Archdiocese of Montréal, (hereafter AAM), Soeurs Grises de Montréal, 1841–1848, file 525.103, document 848–2, Category of the Orphans at Point St. Charles.

[80] ARCAT, St. Paul's Cemetery Register, 1849–1850.

[81] Brian P. Clarke, "Piety and Nationalism: The Rise of Irish Catholic Voluntary Associations in Toronto, 1850–1895" (Ph.D. Dissertation, University of Chicago, 1986), 28.

[82] Poster of *Superior* from Houston & Smyth; selections from *Limerick Chronicle*, 1847.

[83] LAC, Colonial Office 384/80, 197–98.

[84] From a Facsimile of Poster in the rebuilt *Jeanie Johnston*.

[85] *Limerick Chronicle*, 14 April 1847. Credit was given to Captain R. Lynch, R.N., the "emigration agent of this port, as usual particularly active in making passengers as comfortable as possible, amongst whom great order and regularity prevail."

[86] De Vere Testimony, Select Committee, 1847–1848; CO 384/79535 and Arthur Doughty, ed., *The Elgin-Grey Papers, 1846–1852* (Ottawa: J.G. Patenaude, King's Printer, 1937), "Stephen DeVere to Earl Grey, 30 November 1847, London, Canada West," 1341–42.

[87] Robert Whyte, *The Ocean Plague: A Voyage to Quebec in an Irish Emigrant Vessel* (Boston: Coolidge and Wiley, 1848), 46. See also McGowan, "Famine Facts, and Fabrication: An Examination of Diaries from the Irish Famine Migration to Canda," (Forthcoming in *Canadian Journal of Irish Studies*, Spring 2009).

[88] LAC, Colonial Office 384/79, "Letter to the Right Honourable Earl Grey … By the Honourable Adam Ferrie, Member of the Legislative Council," Montréal: *The Pilot*, 1 December 1847.

[89] O'Gallagher, *Eyewitness*, xix.

90 *Limerick Chronicle*, 29 May 1847.

91 Charbonneau, 16.

92 *The Elgin-Grey Papers*, Vol. 1 (Ottawa: J.O. Patenaude, 1937), Elgin to Grey, 13 August 1847, 65.

93 *Pilot and Journal of Commerce* (Montréal), 17 August 1847.

94 AAM, Soeurs Grises de Montréal, 1841–1848, file 525.103, document 847–6, McMullen to Bourget, 7 August 1847.

95 Towns, "Relief and Order," 35.

96 Colin McMahon, "Montreal's Ship Fever Monument: An Irish Famine Memorial in the Making," *Canadian Journal of Irish Studies*, Vol. 33, no. 1 (2007): 48–60.

97 *The Elgin-Grey Papers*, Vol. 1 (Ottawa: J.O. Patenaude, 1937), Elgin to Grey, 13 August 1847, p. 65.

98 *Limerick Reporter*, 19 March 1847.

99 Towns, "Relief and Order," 67.

100 LAC, CO 384/80, "Guidelines," 198.

101 Towns, "Relief and Order," 47; Edwin Guillet.

102 *Globe*, 19 June 1847.

103 *Mirror*, 1 January 1847.

104 *Mirror*, 8 and 16 May 1846.

105 City of Toronto Archive (hereafter CTA), City Council Minutes, 15 March 1847, Motion by Alderman Duggan that fifty pounds be directed to Irish relief.

106 Joy Parr, "The Welcome and the Wake: Attitudes in Canada West Toward Irish Famine Migration," *Ontario History* 66 (1974).

107 *The Church*, 23 April 1847.

108 Archives of the Roman Catholic Archdiocese of Toronto (hereafter ARCAT), Michael Power Papers (hereafter PP), Pastoral Letter, 13 May 1847. See also Mark G. McGowan, *Michael Power: The Struggle to Build the Catholic Church on the Canadian Frontier* (Montréal and Kingston: McGill-Queen's University Press, 2005), 240–3.

109 Macadamization, named for J.L. McAdam, a 19th-century British surveyor, involved building roads by spreading layers of gravel.

110 AO, RG-11-3, Hawke Letterbook, Hawke to Buchanan, 11 April 1847.

111 AO, RG-11-3, A.B. Hawke Papers, Letterbook 1845–1850, Hawke to Buchanan, 21 February 1847 and Hawke to Buchanan, 8 January, 1847.

112 AO, Hawke Letterbook, Hawke to J.H. Palmer (Hamilton), Edward McElderry (Toronto) and G.R. Burke (Bytown), 13 March 1847 and 30 March 1847; Hawke to Buchanan, 11 April 1847.

113 Frederick Armstrong, *Toronto: The Place of Meeting, An Illustrated History* (Toronto: Windsor Publications and the Ontario Historical Society, 1983),89; see also Johnston, *Becoming Prominent: Regional Leadership in Upper Canada, 1791–1841* (Montréal and Kingston: McGill-Queen's University Press, 1989); Frederick Armstrong, "George Gurnett," *Dictionary of Canadian Biography*, Vol IX (1861–1870); Hereward Senior, "William Henry Boulton," *Dictionary of Canadian Biography*, Vol. X (1871–1880).

114 AO, RG-11-3, Hawke Letterbook, Hawke to Buchanan, 15 July 1847;

Hawke to Buchanan, 14 May 1847; Hawke to McElderry, 21 April 1847.

[115] Towns, "Relief and Order," 82.

[116] AO, RG-11-3, Hawke Letterbooks, Hawke to J.E. Campbell, Civil Secretary, 3 June 1847; Hawke to McElderry, 21 April 1847; Hawke to McElderry, 14 May 1847.

[117] AO, Hawke Letterbook, Hawke's Remarks on Mr. Forbes' Letter, 7 May 1847.

[118] CTA, Council Minutes, Report of the Board of Health, 27 May 1847. This was the first report of the Board despite having been established in February.

[119] *British Colonist*, 12 June 1847. AO, Hawke Papers, Copy of Letter, Dominick Daly to W.H. Boulton, 7 June 1847.

[120] Archives of St. James Cathedral, Toronto, John Young Diary, typescript, 13 August 1847.

[121] *British Colonist*, 22 June 1847.

[122] *British Colonist*, 22 June 1847.

[123] AO, Hawke Papers, copy, Quarter Master General, George Ryerson (Montréal) to Boulton. 2 June 1847.

[124] AO, Hawke Papers, copy, General Hospital to C. Daly, 5 June 1847.

[125] *British Colonist*, 22 June 1847.

[126] *British Colonist*, 22 June 1847.

[127] James T. Connor, *Doing Good: The Life of Toronto's General Hospital* (Toronto: University of Toronto Press, 2000), 44.

[128] *Globe*, 23 June 1847.

[129] Mary Larratt Smith, ed. *Young Mr. Smith in Upper Canada* (Toronto: University of Toronto Press, 1980), 111. The letter was written to William Violett, Smith's uncle, 23 June 1847.

[130] Smith, *Young Mr. Smith in Upper Canada*, 111–12.

[131] AO, RG-11-3, Hawke Letterbook, Hawke to Buchanan, 21 September 1847 and 16 October 1847. Hawke indicates that American authorities are not letting the Irish and British migrants into the United States. Steamships on Lake Champlain are refusing the Irish passage from Lower Canada and a border guard at Lewiston, New York, was "imprisoned" for allowing Irish emigrants to land from Upper Canada.

[132] *Globe*, 12 February 1848.

[133] *Limerick Reporter*, 19 March 1847.

[134] *Globe*, 5 August 1847.

[135] AO, RG-11-3, Hawke Letterbook, Hawke to J.E. Campbell, Civil Secretary, 20 September 1847.

[136] *Elgin-Grey Correspondence*, Elgin to Grey, 13 August 1847.

[137] *Globe*, 12 February 1848.

[138] *British Colonist*, 20 August 1847 includes Board of Health Report, 18 August 1847.

[139] *British Colonist*, 20 August 1847.

[140] AO, Hawke Papers, Letterbook, Hawke to McElderry, 15 April 1847. In total Hawke paid his emigrant agents in Bytown (A.R. Burke), Cobourg/Port Hope (A.B. Hawkins), Toronto (E.M. McElderry), and Hamilton (L.P. Palmer) one pound sterling per day. Emigrant physicians were paid variously: Dr. Thomas Robinson (Kingston) £50, Dr. Dickenson (Hamilton) £30, and Dr. Courtland (Bytown) £ 25,

for the entire season (1 May to 1 November). AO, Hawke Papers, Letterbook, 17 April 1847.

[141] AO, Hawke Letterbook, Hawke to Buchanan, 15 July 1847.

[142] AO, Hawke Letterbook, Hawke to the Honourable W. Cayley, Inspector General, 23 November 1847.

[143] AO, Hawke Letterbook, Hawke to Buchanan, 4 August 1847.

[144] LAC, RG 5 C1, Provincial Civil Secretary Papers, Office of the Board of Health, Toronto, to Dominick Daly, 30 August 1847, 4 (Reel C-10802).

[145] *British Colonist*, 3 September 1847.

[146] AO, Hawke Papers, Convalescent Hospital Ledger, lines 315 and 752.

[147] AO, RG 11-1-3, Hawke Letterbook, Hawke to Buchanan, 11 April 1847.

[148] AO, Hawke Papers, Hawke to all Sub Agents, April 1847, 98.

[149] AO, Hawke Papers, Letterbook, Hawke to Sir Thomas Edmund Campbell, 17 April 1847.

[150] *Globe*, 25 August 1847.

[151] *Globe*, 25 August 1847.

[152] Archives of St. James Cathedral, Toronto, John Young Diary, 12 August 1847.

[153] De Vere, as cited in *Elgin-Grey Correspondence*, Vol. IV, 1345.

[154] Archives of St. James Cathedral (Anglican), Grasett Family Papers, George Gurnett to George Grasett, 22 June 1847.

[155] LAC, RG 5 C1, Civil Secretary, Board of Health to Daly, 30 August 1847, 3.

[156] *British Colonist*, 2 November 1847.

[157] There was no standard for sheds in the colonies. In Bytown (Ottawa), according to Grey Sister Mother Elisabeth Bruyère, the government erected sheds 33 feet long and 20 feet wide. (Jeanne D'Arc Lortie, sco, *Lettres de Élisabeth Bruyère* Vol, 1, 1839–1849. Montréal: Éditions Paulines, 1989, 347.) In June, in Toronto, local authorities were using open-sided sheds (*British Colonist*, 25 June 1847); by July it was reported that there were sheds with at least 22 windows each to assist with ventilation (*British Colonist*, 23 July 1847). At Grosse Île, the prefabricated sheds from Quebec City were much larger, with some measuring 408 feet by 25 feet, and a height of ten feet. (André Charbonneau and André Sevigny, *Grosse Île: A Record of Daily Events*, Ottawa: Canadian Heritage – Parks Canada, 1997, 159).

[158] Archives of St. James Cathedral, Grasett Family Scrapbook, Funeral Card, George Grasett.

[159] Archives of St. James Cathedral, Grasett Family Scrapbook, Funeral Card, George Grasett, 2–3.

[160] *British Colonist,* 31 August 1847.

[161] *British Colonist*, 6 August 1847.

[162] Connor, *Doing Good*, 58–59.

[163] *Elgin-Grey Correspondence*, Vol. IV, 1312–1319. One scientist, Colonel Calvert, contracted typhus and died while undertaking experiments at Grosse Île. The two competing solutions for adoption were lead nitrate and zinc chloride. Each was being used in the cleansing of hospital facilities, the bilge water of ships, and ulcerated surfaces on patients.

[164] *British Colonist*, 6 August 1847.

[165] *Mirror*, 19 November 1847.

[166] *Mirror*, 6 August 1847.

[167] *Mirror*, 10 September 1847.

[168] *British Colonist*, 20 July 1847.

[169] Board of Health Regulations, 19 August 1847, as reported in British Colonist, 20 August 1847.

[170] McGowan, *Michael Power*, 173.

[171] *Mirror*, 18 February 1848.

[172] André Charbonneau and Doris Drolet-Dubé, *A Register of the Deceased Persons at Sea and on Grosse Île in 1847* (Ottawa: Canadian Heritage – Parks Canada, 1997), 60 and 99.

[173] *Globe*, 28 July 1847, and Charbonneau and Drolet-Dubé, A Register of Deceased Persons at Sea and on Grosse Île in 1847, 60 and 99.

[174] *The Patriot*, 17 August 1847 and *Toronto Examiner*, 18 August 1847.

[175] *Mirror*, 10 September 1847.

[176] Ontario Genealogical Society, *St. Paul's Roman Catholic Parish, Toronto, Ontario, Burial Records 1842–1857 and Material Related to St. Paul's Cemetery* (Toronto: OGS, 1996), Appendix I E "Fees for Coffins, Conveyances, Grave Digging, Etc."

[177] *British Colonist*, Report of Board of Health, Saturday, August 7, 1847.

[178] AO, Hawke Papers, WB Davis to Mayor Boulton, 28 August 1847.

[179] Censuses of Canada, 1665–1871, Vol. 4 of Census of Canada, 1870–1871 (Ottawa: I.B. Taylor, 1876), 134–5 and 165–6, Table II.

[180] J.M.S. Careless, *Toronto to 1918: An Illustrated History* (Toronto: Lorimer, 1984), 46.

[181] Careless, *Toronto to 1918*, 199.

[182] E.C. Kyte, ed., *Old Toronto: A Selection of Excerpts from "Landmarks of Toronto"* by John Ross Robertson (Toronto: MacMillan, 1954), 98.

[183] Kyte, *Old Toronto*, 95–96.

[184] Kyte, *Old Toronto*, 83–4. Eric Arthur, Toronto: *No Mean City* (Toronto: University of Toronto Press, revised 1986), 47.

[185] Bruce Elliott, "Irish Protestants," in Paul Robert Magosci, ed., *Encyclopedia of Canada's Peoples* (Toronto: University of Toronto Press, 1999): 763–83.

[186] AO, Hawke Papers, Convalescent Hospital Ledger, Toronto, August 1847 to May 1848, Appendix B.

[187] *British Colonist*, 31 August 1847.

[188] *British Colonist*, 13 August 1847.

[189] *British Colonist*, 24 August 1847. McGowan, *Michael Power*, 256.

[190] Robert Scollard, CSB, *They Honoured the Vestments of Holiness: A Calendar of Deceased Bishops, Priests and Deacons of the Archdiocese of Toronto* (Toronto: Archdiocese of Toronto, 1990), 60, 63 and 71.

[191] *British Colonist*, 24 August 1847; McGowan, *Michael Power*, 256.

[192] Archives of the Institute of the Blessed Virgin Mary (hereafter AIBVM), Toronto, Annals, 1847–1870, by Mother Teresa Dease (and transcribed by Maggie Lyons, 25 August 1875), 14.

[193] AIBVM, Annals, 1847–1870, 11.

194 Archives of the Archdiocese of Halifax, William Walsh Papers, Vol. 3, J.J. Hay to William Walsh, 2 October 1847.

195 *The Cross* (Halifax), 23 October 1847; *Mirror*, 8 October 1847; *Mélanges religieux*, 5 October 1847.

196 AO, RG 2-3-5, Ontario Department of Education, Container 1, General Board of Education, Minutes of Meeting (draft), 21 July 1846.

197 *British Colonist*, 13 August 1847.

198 *Mirror*, 5 August 1847.

199 *Mirror*, 2 July 1847.

200 *Globe*, 31 July 1847.

201 AO, Hawke Papers, RG-11-6, Ledger of the Convalescent Hospital; Board of Health Minutes, in *British Colonist*, September 1847.

202 *Mirror*, 5 August 1847. Curtis Fahey, "Charles Donlevy," *Dictionary of Canadian Biography*, Vol. VIII (1851–1860) (Toronto: University of Toronto Pres, 1985).

203 *Mirror*, 20 August 1847.

204 *Mirror*, 19 November 1847.

205 *Mirror*, 20 August 1847.

206 *British Colonist*, 27 August 1847.

207 *Elgin-Grey Correspondence*, Elgin to Grey, 13 July 1847. pp. 58–59.

208 *Toronto Examiner*, 18 August 1847.

209 *Globe*, 4 August 1847.

210 *British Colonist*, 23 July 1847.

211 *British Colonist*, 23 July 1847.

212 AO, Hawke Letterbook, Hawke's Remarks on Mr. Forbes' Letter, 7 May 1847; Report from Kingston, 30 June 1847; Hawke to John A. Macdonald, 12 August 1847; Hawke to Buchanan, 21 September 1847; Hawke to J.E. Campbell, 16 October 1847.

213 AO, Hawke Letterbook, Hawke to J.E. Campbell, Civil Secretary, 20 September 1847.

214 AO, Hawke Letterbook, Hawke to J.E. Campbell, 16 October 1847.

215 *Mirror*, 22 September 1847.

216 AO, Hawke Letterbook, Hawke to J.E. Sullivan, 4 November 1847.

217 AO, Hawke Papers, R.B. Sullivan to George Gurnett, 2 May 1848; "Terrence O'Neil and Samuel G. Lynn to Samuel B. Harrison, Surrogate Court of York", 27 November 1851; *British Colonist*, 11 November 1851.

218 AO, Hawke Papers, Report of the Executive Council to the Honourable Provincial Secretary, 11 October 1847.

219 Towns, "Relief and Order," 95.

220 Towns, "Relief and Order," 97–98.

221 AO, MS 640, Reel 16, Committee for the Asylum, Minute Books, 1846.

222 AO, Hawke Letterbook, Hawke to J.E. Campbell, 27 August 1847 and 20 September 1847.

223 AO, Hawke Letterbook, Estimated Costs of Transportation and Food, to December 1847, p. 190; Board of Health Claims to 23 December 1847, 204.

224 Towns, "Relief and Order," 9. British Parliamentary Papers (hereafter BPP),

Papers Relative to Emigration to the British Provinces in North America, No. 14, Copy of Despatch from Earl of Elgin to Earl Grey, 17 March 1848. Elgin presented total expenses for £138, 781. 6s. 1d. A detailed report can be found in A.C. Buchanan's "Appendix to Report on Emigration, 1847," 21–31. *The Mirror* (26 November 1847) argued that the Home Government ought to be responsible for the Hospital Expenditure, which Donlevy claimed was in excess of £100,000, at least 16 per cent of which had been Toronto's share.

225 *Elgin-Grey Correspondence*, Elgin to Grey, 24 December 1847, I: 102-3 and Grey to Elgin, 14 April 1848, I: 138.

226 BPP, Papers Relative to Emigration to the British Provinces in North America, Enclosure No. 12, "An Act With Respect to Make Better Provision for Emigrants …," (1848) and Enclosure 193, Dispatch from Earl Grey to Lord Elgin, Amendments to the Indigent Immigrant Act, 19 February 1848.

227 *Elgin-Grey Correspondence,* Grey to Elgin, 14 April 1848, I: 138.

228 LAC, Colonial Office Papers, Vol. 384, Buchanan's Report for 1848. There was no crop failure in 1847, but the harvest was meagre and the misery in Ireland continued and was compounded by a return of the blight the following year. Daly, "The Great Famine in Irish Society," 8.

229 Cited in Gilbert Tucker, "The Famine Immigration to Canada, 1847," *American Historical Review* 36 (April 1933): 534. Tucker indicates that in 1848 and 1849, approximately 188,233 and 219,450 migrants from the United Kingdom set sail for the United States.

230 *Mirror*, 18 February 1847.

231 Note Toronto's Archbishop Lynch in the *Irish Canadian*, 25 March 1871.

232 *Irish Canadian*, 7 March 1866.

233 These issues are covered at greater length by Mark G. McGowan, *Creating Canadian Historical Memory: The Case of the Famine Migration of 1847* (Ottawa: Canadian Historical Association, Canada's Ethnic Group Series, Booklet 30, 2006).

234 *British Colonist*, 22 June 1847.

235 *Mirror*, 18 February 1848.

236 *Globe*, 27 September 1848. Also cited in Joy Parr, "The Welcome and the Wake: Attitudes in Canada West Towards the Irish Famine Migration," *Ontario History*, 66 (June 1974): 101–02; Charbonneau and Drolet-Dubé, *A Register of Deceased Persons*, 14 and 66; O'Gallagher, *Eyewitness Grosse Île*, Table 8, 352.

237 AO, RG 10 20-B-4-1/ 150-20-B-4, 5, Queen Street Mental Hospital Papers, Admissions, 1847–48 (MS 640 Reel # 14).

238 *Report of the Managing Committee of the Widows and Orphans' Asylum, for the Care and Maintenance of the Destitute Widows and Orphans of the Emigrants of 1847* (Toronto, 1848).

239 ARCAT, St. Paul's Parish, Spiritual Statistics, Reel 1, April 18, 1848.

240 Toronto Public Library, Baldwin Collection, Booklet, Widows and Orphans Association, "Return of Children and Sent Out to Service," R. McCausland, Superintendent, 30 May 1848.

241 Little research has been done on the Irish orphans at Grosse Île. See O'Gallagher, *Grosse Île: Gateway to Canada*, 56–57 and 117–41.

242 *Mirror*, 18 February 1848.

243 *Mirror*, 18 February 1848.

244 *Careless, Toronto to 1918*, 199.

245 *Censuses of Canada*, 1665–1871, Volume 4 of *Census of Canada*, 1870–1871 (Ottawa: I.B. Taylor, 1876), 165–66, table II.

246 The censuses of 1848 and 1851 as cited in Michael Cottrell, "Political Leadership and Party Allegiance Among Irish Catholics in Victorian Toronto," in McGowan and Clarke, eds., *Catholics at the Gathering Place*, 64.

247 CTA, House of Industry, Fonds 1035, Series 802, File 8, Ledgers from the House of Industry, Toronto, Canada West.

248 CTA, House of Industry, Fonds 1035, Series 802, File 8, Ledgers from the House of Industry, Toronto, Canada West.

249 Murray Nicolson, "Irish Tridentine Catholicism in Victorian Toronto: Vessel for Ethno-Religious Persistence," Canadian Catholic Historical Association, *Study Sessions* 50 (1983), Vol. II: 415–36.

250 J.R. Miller, "Anti-Catholic Thought in Victorian Canada," *Canadian Historical Review* 66 (1985): 474–94; Robert Sylvain, *Alessandro Gavazzi (1809–1889)*, 2 Vols. (Québec: le Centre pédagogique, 1962); Nive Voisine et Jean Hamelin, dirs. *Les Ultramontanes Canadiens-Francais* (Montréal: Boréal Express, 1985).

251 Neil Gregor Smith, "Religious Tensions in Pre-Confederation Politics," *Canadian Journal of Theology* 9 (October 1963): 248–62; John S. Moir, "The Origins of the Separate School Question in Ontario," *Canadian Journal of Theology* 2 (1959): 105–18; John S. Moir, "Toronto's Protestants and Their Perceptions of Their Roman Catholic Neighbours," in Mark G. McGowan and Brian P. Clarke, eds., *Catholics at the Gathering Place: Historical Essays on the Archdiocese of Toronto, 1841–1991* (Toronto: CCHA and Dundurn Press, 1993): 313–27; Roberto Perin, "Elaborating a Public Culture: The Catholic Church in Nineteenth Century Quebec," in Marguerite Van Die, ed., *Religion and Public Life in Canada; Historical and Comparative Perspectives* (Toronto: University of Toronto Press, 2001): 87–105.

252 LAC, Sir John A. Macdonald Papers, MG 26A, Vol. 188 (1872), "The History of Roman Catholics in Canada," 78665–78686. The quotation is attributed to George Brown, editor of the Toronto *Globe*, although no date is offered in the pamphlet, where it appears on page 78666. Given that the pamphlet was produced by the Conservative Party to discredit the Liberal Party and its leader, George Brown, to Catholic voters, one must be suspicious as to whether the statement could be attributed to Brown. The rest of the pamphlet is filled with anti-Catholic and some anti–Irish Catholic comments, with corresponding dates in the *Globe* or publication details elsewhere by Brown and other members of his party. The most cited reference for the statement is *Globe*, 11 February 1858. Unfortunately, the issue in question does not include the quotation, nor do any issues in months preceding or following the issue in question. In the pamphlet it appears that the quotation was derived from a public speech that Brown allegedly made.

253 Mark G. McGowan, *The Waning of the Green: Catholics, the Irish and Identity in Toronto, 1887–1922* (Montréal and Kingston: McGill-Queen's University Press, 1999).

254 Coined in John S. Moir, "The Problem of a Double Minority: Some Reflections

on the Development of the English-speaking Catholic Church in Canada in the Nineteenth Century," *Histoire sociale—Social History* 4 (April 1971): 53–67.

255 Simon Jolivet, "Les deux questions irlandaises du Québec, 1898–1921: des considerations canadiennes-françaises et irlando-catholiques," (Ph.D. dissertation, Concordia University, 2008).

256 O'Gallagher, *Grosse Île*, 86.

257 Canadian Heritage-Parks Canada, *Grosse Île and the Irish Quarantine Tragedy: Report of the Advisory Panel (Québec, August 1995). Grosse Île: Development Concept* (Ottawa: Ministry of the Environment, 1992); *Montreal Gazette*, 21 May 1992; *Toronto Star*, 10 October 1992; *Globe and Mail*, 21 August 1989.

258 Montreal *Gazette*, 19 August 1994.

259 Ireland Park Foundation, "Objectives and Fundraising Goals," Ireland Park, Toronto, Brochure, 2007.

260 Yvonne Whelan and Liam Harte, "Placing Geography in Irish Studies: Symbolic Landscapes of Spectacle and Memory," in Whelan and Harte, eds., *Ireland Beyond Boundaries: Mapping Irish Studies in the Twenty-First Century* (London: Pluto Press, 2007), 175–97. On page 191, Harte and Whelan are clear: "As Famine memorials were added to a number of cityscapes … commentators were quick to note the way in which the Famine Irish were co-opted into the American dream. At many of these commemorative sites, the past is scripted as a triumphant journey from penury to socio-economic success, typically through the depiction of family groups departing Ireland in various states of emaciation and despair, only to arrive in America with hearts full of purposeful hope." Harte and Whelan remark, however, that Brian Tolle's Irish Hunger Memorial in New York is very different. It "at once evokes and interrogates the metaphysics of home and the memory that haunts the migrant imaginary." (192) A reconstructed ruined Famine cottage from Mayo, it forces the viewer to come to terms with the Famine, individually, without the suggestions posed by other memorializations in the United States. "It's about the experience you're having right now. 'It's about you' … viewers are invited to contemplate both the necessity of remembrance and the irretrievability of the past, to meditate on both history itself and their own relationship to that history." (195)

261 Peter Gray, "Memory and the Great Irish Famine," in Peter Gray and Kendrick Oliver, eds., *The Memory of Catastrophe* (Manchester: Manchester University Press, 2004), 53. One of the leading scholars on Famine memory is James Donnelly; see the final chapter in his *The Great Irish Potato Famine* (Phoenix Mill, UK: Sutton Publishing, 2001). Also of note are Mick Mulcrone, "The Famine and Collective Memory: The Role of the Irish-American Press in the Early Twentieth Century" in Arthur Gribben, ed., *The Great Irish Famine and the Irish Diaspora in America* (Boston: University of Massachusetts Press, 1999): 219–38 and R.F. Foster, *The Irish Story: Telling Tales and Making It Up in Ireland* (London: Penguin, 2001).

262 Gray, "Memory and the Great Irish Famine," 55.

263 Campbell, *The Great Irish Famine*, 54–55.

264 AO, Hawke Letterbook, Remarks on Mr. Forbes' Letter, 7 May 1847.

265 Toronto *Mirror*, 18 February 1847

266 ARCAT, Alexander Macdonell Papers, AB01.02 James Baby to Macdonell, May 1822, two notes.

267 ARCAT, Macdonell Papers, AB01.07, Baby to Macdonell, 2 February 1824.

268 John R. Teefy, Jubilee Volume (Toronto: George T. Dixon, 1892): 285.

269 Teefy, Jubilee Volume, 98–99.

270 Teefy, Jubilee Volume, 287.

271 ARCAT, Macdonell Papers, CB09.03, Regulations of the Catholic Mission of Toronto, c.1831.

272 ARCAT, Macdonell Papers, CB09.03, Regulations of the Catholic Mission of Toronto, c.1831.

273 Eric Wilfrid Hounsom, Toronto in 1810 (Toronto: Ryerson Press, 1970): 120.

274 ARCAT, Macdonell Papers, CB09.03, Regulations of the Catholic Mission of Toronto, c.1831.

275 McGowan, Michael Power, 145–46 and Murray Nicolson, "William O'Grady and the Catholic Church in Toronto Prior to the Irish Famine," in McGowan and Clarke, eds., Catholics at the Gathering Place, 23–40.

276 ARCAT, Macdonell Papers, AC32.06, Detailed Accounts, 1832.

277 ARCAT, Macdonell Papers, AB18.03, John Elmsley to Macdonell, 11 March 1836.

278 Michael Harrison, St. Paul's Roman Catholic Parish, Burial Records, 1842–1857 (Toronto: OGS, 1996), viii–xiii.

279 Hounsom, Toronto in 1810, 119.

280 ARCAT, St. Paul's Parish Box, Census Form, William P. McDonough, c.1834–1842.

281 Michael Katz, The People of Hamilton, Canada West: Family and Class in a Mid-Nineteenth-Century City (Cambridge: Cambridge University Press, 1975); David Gagan, Hopeful Travellers: Families, Land and Social Change in Mid-Victorian Peel County, Canada West (Toronto: University of Toronto Press, 1981).

282 ARCAT, CC SP01.02, Armand de Charbonnel Papers, James Fitzgerald to Charbonnel, 5 July 1852.

283 McGowan, Michael Power, 173.

284 McGowan, Michael Power, 285.

285 Harrison, St. Paul's Roman Catholic Parish, Burial Records, 1842–1857, 234.

286 While this method is problematic, it does help to fill in the gaps created by the omission of a person's place of birth.

287 This slip of paper would make an excellent visual for filmmakers—ironically, the list was printed on the back of an invitation to a "Social Assembly" held January 24, 1849. The "Ball and Refreshments" cost each participant five shillings. ARCAT, CC SP01.01.

288 British Colonist, 31 August 1847.

289 Edward Kelly, The Story of St. Paul's, Toronto, 1822–1922 (Toronto, 1922), 97.

290 Board of Health Regulations, 19 August 1847, as reported in British Colonist, 20 August 1847.

291 ARCAT, St. Paul's Parish, Financial and Legal, 1832–1891, Board of Health to Wardens (Hayes and Higgins), c. December 1, 1847. The number 34 was calculated by dividing the bill by 33.2 shillings, which appeared as the average

cost of burial per person in December (5 interments for £8 6s).

[292] Topographical Plan of the City of Toronto in the Province of Canada from actual survey of Stoughton Dennis, Provincial Land Surveyor, 1851. Drawn and Compiled by Sanford A. Fleming. NMC 8653. Referenced in John R. Triggs, *An Investigation into St. Paul's Catholic Cemetery, 80 Sackville Street, Toronto* (Toronto: Historic Horizon Inc., 1998), Figure 1.

[293] ARCAT, St. Paul's File, Indenture, Episcopal Corporation of the Archdiocese of Toronto to the Toronto Catholic School Board, 30 January 1959.

[294] ARCAT, Charbonnel Papers, Fitzgerald to Charbonnel, 5 July 1852.

[295] *Jubilee Volume*, 221.

[296] Archives of the Congregation of the Sisters of St. Joseph, Toronto (hereafter ACSSJ), *Annals of the House of Providence*, 3.

[297] ACSSJ, *Annals of the House of Providence*, 9. ARCAT, Charbonnel Papers, SP 01.03, "Public Notice [Father J.M. Soulerin, csb, Administrator]," 1857. No interments were permitted after June 1, 1857.

[298] *Annals*, 21.

[299] ARCAT, CC SP02.01, Petition to the Archbishop, c. 1870.

[300] *Jubilee Volume*, 286.

[301] Kelly, *The Story of St. Paul's*, 185.

[302] ACSSJ, *Highlights in Our History: House of Providence, Providence Villa and Hospital, Providence Centre, Fact Sheet* page 1.

[303] Kelly, *The Story of St. Paul's*, 186; John Ross Robertson, *Landmarks of Toronto: A Collection of Historical Sketches from the Old Town of York from 1792–1837* (Toronto: Evening Telegram, 1906), Vol. 5.

[304] *Annals*, 75.

[305] *Globe*, 10 October 1932 and *Toronto Star*, 11 October 1932. See also *Catholic Register*, 6 and 13 October 1932. The *Register* includes the entire text of O'Donnell's homily.

[306] Correspondence with historian Michael Power, who has an unpublished manuscript on the history of the parish.

[307] ACSSJ, House of Providence, Letter from H.R. Dillon, Assistant Manager, Real Estate Department, City of Toronto, to Honourable Frank J. Hughes (lawyer for CSJ), 18 December 1961. Details are given of the transfer of 170,400 square feet of land, bounded by Power Street on the west and Sackville Street on the east. (439.82 feet along Power Street, 229.52 along Sackville Street, 543.80 feet of a northern but irregular boundary [facing school and diocesan lands], and 532 feet of land as southern boundary.

[308] CTA, Folder Box 800046-8, Series 3, File 125, 1960–1964, Aerial Photographs of Richmond Street and Adelaide Street Ramp Construction. Photo ES14-10 clearly indicates Bosco Hall near the new St. Paul's School building, and other photos indicate heavy fill applied to the area.

[309] ARCAT, St. Paul's Cemetery File, Indenture, 30 January 1959.

[310] ARCAT, SP01.04, Arthur Kelly to Father Thomas J. Fulton, 17 June 1959.

[311] ARCAT, James McGuigan Papers, SC 25.03, Matthew Dymond to McGuigan, 29

June 1959.

[312] ARCAT, St. Paul's Parish Box, Father W. O'Brien to Philip Pocock, 21 October 1963.

[313] Triggs, 9–16.

[314] The Ireland Fund of Canada ("The Jubilant Man"); Hurley Corporation ("The Pregnant Woman"); The Ireland Canada Chamber of Commerce ("Woman on the Ground"); The Patrick's Benevolent Society of Toronto ("The Orphan Boy"); Oliver Murray ("The Apprehensive Man").

[315] A list of donors is located on the Ireland Park website.

Index

DEATH or CANADA

"An extraordinary tribute   to the human spirit."

NARRATED BY BRIAN DENNEHY

www.deathorcanada.com

An epic docudrama produced by Ballinran Productions and Tile Films in association with Canwest Broadcasting, RTE Ireland, and The History Channel UK